D0001508

Scott
PUBLICATIONS

SCOTT PUBLICATIONS
30595 EIGHT MILE
LIVONIA, MI 48152-1798

Copyright ©1992
Library of Congress #92-080754
ISBN #0-916809-56-0

No. 3137-5-92
PRINTED IN USA

Cover: Very rare No. 223 Jumeau Character. 24".

Fabulous French Bébés

FOR COLLECTORS AND CRAFTERS

Three Brus (also shown undressed on page 136) are dressed in original costumes. Larger doll has blue eyes and small dolls have brown eyes. Wigs are original.

By Mildred Seeley

in cooperation with Vernon Seeley

Photography: Mildred Seeley and Kay Manley Studios

Table of Contents

Left: Two Brevetés, made by Bru, 13'' and 12''. Both dolls wear original sheepskin wigs.

Right: E.J.8., 18". Nice even-toned dark skinned Jumeau.

How to Become a Bébé Collector

An old doll is part of the memory of our childhood. Dolls were designed in the heart and made by hand with love. Now, as adults, we collect and protect these treasures from our past.

Doll collecting is a passion that involves over a half-million adults. People collect all types of dolls, from modern plastics to wood dolls made in the 1700s.

It is not difficult to understand why collectors become so involved in collecting dolls. Many of us had one or more dolls when we were children, and men and women have stories to tell about how a doll affected their childhood.

The pinnacle in doll collecting is to possess a *French Bébé* or a collection of *Bébés*. These are the most beautiful, most sought-after, highest-priced dolls available to collectors. Bébés have universal appeal, and they are the dolls most often used for investment.

In this book, we deal with recognizing and collecting these fine French dolls. When we talk about "dolls," we are really discussing *doll heads*. The bodies are important, but they could be changed or left unmarked. So references to French dolls and Bébés is generally a reference to the *head*.

Bébés (pronounced *bay-bays*, with the accent on the last syllable) are dolls with bisque heads, jointed composition bodies or leather child-shaped, jointed bodies. French Bébés were made to represent children. At first, they represented French children. As doll-making companies expanded their markets, they made child dolls to represent many different races.

Today, many collectors use the word Bébé, but more often they use the term *French dolls* for these large-eyed French creations depicting children. In this book, we use the terms interchangeably.

Even though we concentrate on French Bébés (we do not cover French lady dolls made before the Bébés), our suggestions, insights, hints and advice on collecting and using dolls can be applied to *any* bisque doll.

This book will help you recognize French dolls and will help you select and purchase them with confidence. We hope you will learn what to look for in body form, bisque, hands, feet, mouths and markings. We want you to be aware of the workmanship of different companies and to understand variations in a line of dolls because of growth or change within a company.

We provide clear, detailed photos to use for

Left: Bru Jne 8 is 10 inches tall. Good paperweight eyes are always an asset. Blond mohair wig is original. Note mismatched brows, which are often found on Brus.

painting. We also want to provide visual joy for those who only want to look at or study our dolls. We share our collection with you in the hopes of preserving a part of doll history.

INTRIGUE OF DOLL COLLECTING

Collecting French Bébés has the same elements of other good hobbies—it's intriguing, exciting, time consuming, relaxing, friendly and fun. It can also be a good investment.

Collecting dolls may start with a dream, a picture of a fine doll or perhaps a memory of one you had or wanted as a child. This dream or memory leads to the desire to possess that doll or one like it.

The Desire—A beginning collector forms a picture in her mind of a doll she desires. The picture adds a new dimension to her life, and she dreams of the doll as her own.

The Search—The collector sets out to find a particular doll or a similar one. In most hobbies, this is defined as the *search*.

In the search, there are numerous benefits. The collector discovers books about dolls, and in the books she may find photographs of dolls similar to the one she dreams about. Her longest-lasting discovery may be the wonderful people who collect dolls, and she may become friends with many collectors.

Her next discovery is the business of dolls— how to be successful buying and selling them. The collector learns about doll auctions, doll conventions and doll dealers. These are exciting new dimensions in her life.

As she studies books on dolls, the collector's life takes on new excitement. In her spare time, she goes to auctions and sales, learning about dolls and searching for that "special" one for her.

The Chase—After studying dolls and learning about them, the collector knows what she wants and what she is looking for. Her dream becomes a doll with a name. She proceeds to the *chase*, and purchasing a particular doll is her dream.

The Catch—The chase ends with the *catch* when the collector finally buys the doll. She has done a careful job and feels delighted, happy and successful as she holds her treasure. The joy of possession has become a reality.

The collector has progressed from desire, search, chase and catch to possession. These are the same steps followed in nearly every successful collecting hobby.

In doll collecting, the process repeats itself as the collector adds to her collection. Doll collecting may continue for a lifetime, or it may be short-lived. Usually, "once a doll collector, always a doll collector."

IN PURSUIT OF OUR MARQUE DOLLS

The process of desire, search, chase, catch and possession is perfectly illustrated by our search for our two Marque dolls. One of our books on dolls, the Colemans' *The Collector's Encyclopedia of Dolls,* published by Crown Publishers, had a picture of a doll that bore only the signature *A. Marque.* The doll was different, with a pixielike face and large ears, and it always intrigued us.

I don't know if we opened the book to that page so often that the book was worn or whether it was fate. But whenever we used the book, it opened to the picture of the Marque doll, and that was the beginning of our dream.

We were on a trip far from home when we found a sign for a doll museum. We couldn't get in because it was closed, so we waited until the next day, but it was still closed. We found a caretaker, and he took us on a hurried trip through the interior, where we saw many dolls. In the middle of the cases, we found two Marque dolls—a boy doll and girl doll. It was like a dream come true—we immediately fell in love with them!

We knew we *had* to have at least one Marque doll in our collection. The next day, after we had traveled 800 miles farther, we called the owner of the museum, Gaynell Denson, but she wasn't interested in selling either doll at any price.

So we began our search. We knew what we wanted—our doll had a name. We started a notebook of clues. We telephoned the woman whose doll was pictured in the Coleman book. The doll had been sold. We tracked down the doll shop from which the ones in the museum had been purchased in the 1930s. The doll shop was gone and the owner had died, but we discovered she had owned five or six pairs of Marque dolls. We felt there must be at least that many in the United States.

Right: Beautiful doll is incised *Bru Jne 6.* Bru Bébés appeal to many collectors.

Each time a Marque doll was mentioned in articles or talks, we wrote it down and tracked down the owner. We picked up clues and finally located eight Marque dolls. Unfortunately, all the owners were happy with them and had no desire to sell. Our search continued for many years.

About 10 years after we first saw "our" Marque dolls, we received a telephone call. The caller said she knew of a dealer who had a Marque—not in very good condition and without clothing—that was for sale for around $30,000.

Before we contacted the dealer, we took a chance and again called Gaynell Denson at the museum. We caught her at the right time. She wanted to buy a piece of property, and selling a Marque doll would provide the necessary cash. She agreed to sell one doll but said we would have to come and get it because she didn't want to be responsible for shipping it. It meant a four-day trip for us and we had to use the last of our savings to invest in our hobby, but we did it.

We chose the boy doll and named him André. He was exactly as we had dreamed—perfect and in original costume. Gaynell promised to save the girl doll for us if we could come up with enough cash within two years. We did and made the trip again to buy the beautiful doll, which we named Alyce.

We have never regretted buying our two Marque dolls. We have grown to love them more each year. But our story didn't end with buying them. We have used their pictures in our books. We made one mold of the doll and sold limited editions of the reproduction, and we sold molds of smaller sizes. Both dolls have been used on our limited-edition plates.

Our Marque dolls have enriched our lives and have added a new, exciting dimension to our hobby. In our possession, we have something more than a toy or plaything, more than the realization of a dream, more than a bit of history — our Marque dolls are truly fine works of art. For more information on Marque dolls, see the section that begins on page 54.

Marque girl doll, 22", sculpted in 1913.

Albert Marque boy doll, 22"

Left: Our Albert Marque dolls, *Alyce* and *Andre,* are both 22" tall and wear original clothing. We spent 10 years in pursuit of these extremely rare dolls.

Selecting French Dolls

Established doll collectors have their own ideas about how to select a French doll. The following ideas are guidelines to help you recognize and select a French Bébé.

The value or actual selling price of a doll depends on many things. Certain dolls, or types of dolls, sell for high prices, but prices may change from year to year. Trends vary across the country, and certain types of dolls are popular in certain parts of the country.

Beauty is the most important factor to us, but for other collectors, character or an unusual face may be more appealing. We feel a doll is valuable if it's beautiful, like a painting or sculpture. The *mark of the maker*, sculptor or producer is also important.

Good workmanship on a doll is essential. A doll cannot be valuable if it is not well-made. It should be carefully painted, have well-cut eye holes and a head and body that are in good proportion.

Rare dolls are more valuable. If there are only a few dolls to collect, they are considered "rare," and many people will want to add one to their collection. A good doll collection should always contain at least *one* rare doll.

The *general condition* of the doll is also important. If a doll wears her original outfit, she is worth more. If her head and body are in excellent condition, she will have a higher value than a doll with a hairline crack.

Sometimes *uniqueness* is important. Experimental dolls were made by every company. If we find a doll that is truly different, it is bound to be a collector's doll.

If a doll has all, or most, of these qualities, it is worth collecting. Some qualities are more important to some collectors than to other collectors. That's why nearly every doll is sold at a doll auction—there is something about each doll that appeals to a buyer.

DATING FRENCH DOLLS

One of the mistakes made by new collectors of French dolls or people who own only one doll is the attempt to date a doll exactly. They feel they need to know the day, month and year a particular doll was made. *Exact dating* is impossible, as you will understand when you study the way dolls were created and produced, beginning on page 109.

Dolls were made in a production line even in 1885. Hundreds of heads were cast at the same time. When doll heads came out of the fire, they were matched with bodies. Eventually dolls were wigged and costumed. In this production-

Left: Portrait Jumeau is 19 inches tall. Early Bébés like this one resembled lady dolls with thin brows, mauve eye shadow and two-toned lip painting. Eyes of these dolls were more almond-shaped.

line process, it could take several months to produce a particular doll. By the time the doll was advertised, boxed and shipped, even more time had elapsed.

To make a doll, the head had to be first modeled by an artist. The artist probably sculpted heads for *next year's* production. From the time the idea for a doll was conceived until a child received it for Christmas, a few years could have elapsed.

Once production of a certain doll started, it could continue for 10 or 15 years. Production could stop, then start up again, as sales demanded. Consider the Long-Faced Jumeau. It was produced from about 1878 until after 1890. We don't know if it was in continuous production or not.

As far as dating your doll to January 5, 1886, it cannot be done. It's better to generalize and say *very early* dolls, *early* dolls or *late* dolls, as doll dealers do.

There are some things you can recognize instantly that will give you a general idea of the age of the doll. We have listed some of these in the box below.

These are only *general* indications of the time a doll was made. Companies changed the way they did things when they changed to newer methods. Often a company produced a doll for years, using the same method they had used for that doll in the beginning. They did this because production methods had already been established. An example of this is applied ears. Even though a company was pouring other head molds with ears in the mold, it may have continued with the old method of applied ears for a particular doll because head molds were already being used that had ears in a separate mold. They could not change the procedure without having to redesign the doll head.

One excellent way to establish dates should not be overlooked. Often families have histories of their dolls. They know exactly, to the year and day, when Grandmother received a particular doll. Recently we purchased a doll from a neighbor. She received her doll when her brother was born, so she knew the *exact* date. Anyone purchasing dolls from an original owner or relative should check for known dates. Occasionally a note is found with a doll.

Another way to date dolls is to find a particular doll in a reprint of an antique catalog. Labels on bodies with dates indicate only the date after which the doll was made. Dates on shoes indicate the same thing. Published patent dates are as helpful as advertising dates.

HOW TO DETERMINE IF A DOLL IS FRENCH

Some people can look at a doll and say they know it is French or it is not French. When it gets down to it, most people are not that good at

Dating Dolls

VERY EARLY	EARLY	LATE
pressed bisque	label stamped on neck	poured bisque
pale bisque	jointed wrists	orange-toned lips
mauve eye shadow	black lashes	deep-toned bisque
thin brows	definite pattern in	sleep eyes
pale lips	brow painting	open mouth
straight wrists	ears made in mold	no eye shadow or
applied ears	human-hair wigs	only gray or brown
sheepskin wig	fine composition bodies	teeth
unevenly cut eye holes		poor bodies
some wood bodies		

Right: Early Jumeau marked E J A 12, 26''. The A model has a very different face. Her seagreen silk dress is trimmed with blue and most unusual silk chenile and mother of pearl designs at waist and sleeves. A rare doll.

Clowns incised with an anchor and LC. 14". Clothes deteriorating. Probably made by Leconte, Paris.

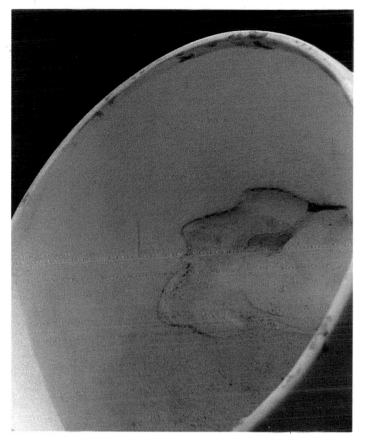

Porcelain rim of French doll head is usually thin, with no reinforcement, and may be warped.

detecting the make of a doll at a glance. It's better to take a little time and study characteristics that will help you decide.

After studying and handling many dolls, your experience will give you confidence about recognizing French dolls. But it is better to examine the doll for markings on the body and head.

Markings—Today, many books are available that help identify doll markings. Before you get too involved in dolls, you should be able to recognize common markings. See the comparison of various markings beginning on page 156. Books and experts can also help identify strange or unfamiliar marks you may sometimes find.

Doll companies seemed to change their markings every few years. For instance, Jumeau had a dozen different ways to mark dolls and bodies. The length of time a company was in business affected the number of markings the company used.

Markings, which are incised (pressed into), in relief (raised above the surface) or stamped with china paint on the back of the head, are very reliable. Body marks are good, except a body could have been changed or painted. Marked shoes or clothing may be an indication of the maker, but these could also have been changed.

The best indication of a French doll is the well-known mark of the maker or the word *Paris* or *France* on the head. The letters *dep* are often incised in a doll, and some people feel this indicates the doll is French. But the mark was

used to mean "registered" by French and German doll makers.

If you buy a doll that is marked with Bru, Jumeau, Steiner or the mark of any other famous French doll maker, you are buying a French doll. The doll will have desired characteristics and should increase in value. She will probably always be a desired *objet d'art*. We feel it is wiser to buy a marked doll.

Eyes—The eyes of the French Bébé should be paperweight, with clear crystal over the center of the eye to give it depth. There can be exceptions, such as when a doll was made before paperweight eyes were invented. If the doll is a wire-eyed Steiner, there will be no crystal bulge because the eyes could not close over a bulge.

Paperweight eyes were not used in later French dolls that had sleep eyes because the eyes would not close. But you still can say, "*Most* dolls with paperweight eyes are French."

Heads—Usually French dolls have a sliced-off head cut on a slant to the back. There is no extra thickness on this rim, only the thickness of the porcelain. See photo above. The open part of the head was covered with a *pate*.

German dolls usually have cardboard pates under their wigs, while French dolls have cork pates. But not all French dolls have cork pates. Steiner dolls had a heavy papier-mâché pate. Schmitt dolls had a flesh-colored, cardboard pate. Pates could have been changed over the years. People often put new cork pates on French dolls, regardless of the make of the doll.

Many German dolls have holes in the sides or back of the head to tie sleep eyes for shipping. Sleep eyes have a weight that swings back and forth, and the weight could crack the porcelain. String was tied around the weight and through the holes. A child's mother cut the string so the eyes would work. French dolls do not have these holes. An exception to this rule is the sleep-eyed SFBJ dolls.

French dolls sometimes have a bald or closed head with two or three holes. Dolls with closed heads are usually referred to as *Belton type*. Holes were used to tie on the wig and to string the doll. Wire on the end of elastic from the legs came up through the neck and through one of the holes. It was bent down through another hole. It was an inexpensive, inferior way to string a doll.

Ears—Applied ears are an indication a doll is French. To date, we have found no exceptions. Pierced ears usually indicate a French doll, but occasionally we also find a German doll with pierced ears.

Mouths—Most people think if a doll has a closed mouth, it is French. The closed mouth is a good indication a doll is French, but there are many exceptions. German doll-making companies made some closed-mouth dolls, such as the Simon & Halbig Nos. 919, 929 and 949. Kämmer & Reinhardt made many dolls with closed mouths, as did other doll makers.

On the other hand, A. Thuillier and Steiner made open-mouthed dolls with two rows of teeth. Even Jumeau made a doll with two rows of teeth. We should say, "The most-desirable French dolls have closed mouths."

Bodies—The bodies of French and German dolls are different. The French doll body is stocky and well-formed, with large hands and feet. The German body is thin, hands are tiny and hands and feet are out of proportion. Early French bodies had unjointed wrists, but later

Belton-type doll, 17 inches tall, marked *1* with an *R* on stem of 1. Maker is unknown.

jointed wrists were made. The German doll body had loose ball-joints, as did the early Jumeau bodies. Later, French doll makers did not use loose ball-joints in the hips, shoulders, arms and knees.

Costumes—Original French clothing can be an indication a doll is French. But you must realize clothing could have been changed.

What to Look for—To summarize, look for the following things in a French doll:

- Markings
- Paperweight eyes
- Pressed porcelain
- Unbroken, unjointed wrists
- Sliced-off head
- Cork pate
- Applied ears
- Pierced ears
- Closed mouth
- Original French clothing

There are exceptions to this list. It's wise to buy marked heads, but there have been exceptions even with these. Some Jumeau heads, such as the Portrait Jumeau and Long-Faced Jumeau, are marked only with numbers. Some A.T. and Bru dolls are marked only on the shoulderplate. If a leather body has disintegrated and the head is put on a composition body, all identification is lost, and the head is considered unmarked.

Right: Incised *France SFBJ 247 Paris*, doll is 28 inches tall and sometimes called the *Twirp*. This later doll has real lashes and sleep eyes. He has an open-closed mouth.

DAMAGED DOLLS

As a collector, you must decide how much damage you can tolerate on a doll. If you want to collect dolls from the latter half of the 19th and the beginning of the 20th centuries, you probably won't find many dolls in original costumes, in original boxes or in original condition. Dolls passed from one generation to the next were not always well-cared for, and certain materials cannot be preserved.

As collectors, we have learned to accept an unclothed doll or a doll in clothing that is too deteriorated to save. We all must understand that these dolls were made a hundred years ago.

We do not recommend to any collector that he or she buy a doll for investment purposes if it has a crack or chip. Today, with more people collecting and only the same number of old dolls being collected, you may have to accept a minor crack, as many European collectors do.

When we began collecting, we decided not to buy a doll if there was *any* damage to the head. After years of collecting, we discovered this kept us from having some very nice dolls and made us wait many years to see a particular doll again.

We've mellowed and can now put a lovely doll with a tiny hairline crack down the back of the head into our cabinet and love her as if she were perfect. We've even had some second thoughts on investment dolls. "Never," we used to say, "buy a doll with even a nick as an investment doll."

But old dolls are scarce, so again we changed our attitude. We believe even if a doll isn't perfect, it can be an investment. If it's a good example of a particular type of doll, if it is a rare doll or if it has some unique feature, it can *still* increase in value.

There are, and always will be, people who see a doll's chipped finger or an oxide fleck on her cheek instead of her beauty. These people would make fine doll collectors *if* they could find anything to collect.

The wonderful French Bébé, created from clay, vitrified by fire and touched with color, is a work of art to be cherished and preserved. But you must realize that after a century of children's love, she may not be perfect.

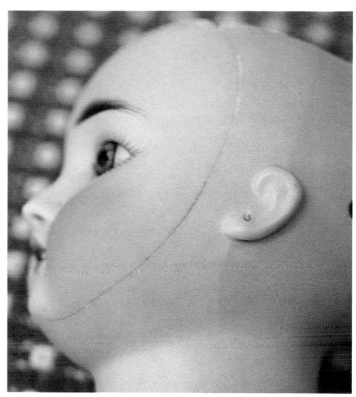
Dolls with face cracks, like this Steiner, are not worth much.

REPAIRED DOLLS

If you select an expensive French doll, you will want to know what repairs it has had, where they are and how extensive they are. Usually you can take the word of a reputable dealer, but the dealer may not have had time to completely go over the doll. Maybe the dealer took the word of someone else.

It's better to see for yourself, and make your own judgments. We're not saying never buy a repaired doll, but we feel you must know *what* repairs a doll has had. Keep in mind that dolls were toys. Unplayed-with dolls are rare.

Bodies—A doll's body is the part that is most often repaired. Papier-mâché or composition bodies often show wear at the joints. Sometimes bodies wear so much that sections crack out. Occasionally dolls were strung too tightly, and the hip joint or neck joint was pulled into the body. Fingers and toes may be cracked or broken off.

We bought one doll, which came from the attic, that had holes in the center of both lower legs. Around the holes were red crayon and the

Bébé Français marked B 10 F, 23". Dressed in antique silk and lace dress.

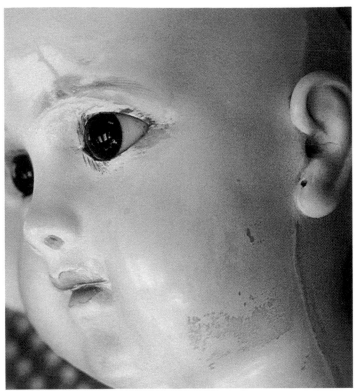
Heads damaged beyond repair, such as this one, can be used to make molds.

remains of old, cloth adhesive tape. This reminded us of how we played hospital when we were children. We thought the tape and red crayon made the holes amusing. Things like this help remind us that dolls were toys.

Sometimes repairs are made neatly—holes filled and the surface repainted where necessary. Joints can be reinforced without greatly decreasing the value of the doll. The poorest repairs seem to be on the replacement of fingers. We have some dolls in our cabinet with finger repairs that were not well-done.

Be careful about choosing a doll with repairs that show when the doll is dressed. Be aware that some repairs may not hold up. Replaced parts are not considered damage, but we consider them less-desirable than damaged parts.

All-over painting of the body is *not* desirable. In the past, many doll hospitals painted any doll brought in, and we have seen many of them. We can't remove the paint, and because these dolls are not being made today, we accept what we cannot change.

If a body on a doll is too big or too small, and obviously wrong, change the body. If you can't

find an old body, put the head on a new body of the right size until you find an old one. The doll will be more pleasant to look at.

Test body elastic by gently pulling on a leg. Is elastic firm or must it be replaced immediately? If you do your own stringing, it should make little difference in the price of the doll.

When a body part is missing, such as an arm or leg, replace *both* arms or legs so they match. If you are thinking about buying an old doll with a leg that has been replaced, you must realize you will never find one to match.

In addition to papier-mâché and composition bodies, leather bodies were also made. These can be ruined by bad repairs. Trying to resew old leather often makes it worse and tears the leather more. The fact that a lot of sawdust or ground cork is gone is minor—it can be replaced. Some bodies are in such bad shape they aren't worth anything, but you must be the judge.

Body and limb repairs are usually obvious. You don't have to be a great detective to see roughness in the finish, a change in the color of paint or a crooked lump that is supposed to be a finger. You should be able to locate repairs on a body by looking. If you can't find them, it doesn't matter.

Feet—When considering a doll, take off shoes, socks and other clothing. You may be shocked to find toes are missing or there is other hidden damage.

Bru dolls often have wood lower legs and feet. These should *not* be repainted. Bru dolls may also have their toes broken off, so be sure to look at their bare feet.

Hands — Bru dolls, and sometimes Jumeaus and Steiners, had bisque hands. Broken fingers are common and are the most difficult parts to replace. Usually, broken fingers are replaced with another material, such as bread dough or epoxy. See *Doll Costuming,* also by Scott Publications, for information on repairing broken fingers and making other repairs.

Most replacements are obvious if you look closely. Sometimes whole hands have been replaced with reproduction hands. Hands on Bru dolls are a part of their charm. Replacing bisque hands greatly decreases the value of a doll, and this should be reflected in the price.

Right: A-series Steiner, 28 inches tall, wears original clothing on her composition body. Fingers are usual for a Steiner—they are all short and about the same size.

Heads—Usually repairs to body parts are minor compared to repairs to a bisque head. Large head repairs or breaks are serious because they decrease the value of a doll. For investment purposes, a doll with extensive head repairs is worth little. It will not increase in value as will French dolls in good condition.

To buy a head and later find it is cracked is an unsettling experience, especially for an advanced collector. Most cracks can be seen if the head is held so strong light shines through it.

Many dealers and auction houses use black lights. In a dark room, a black light pierces the porcelain and shows every crack and repair. When using black lights, we have found repaired cracks that were not otherwise visible. These lights are used for viewing the fluorescence in rock specimens and for stage effects. They are available in many hardware and lighting stores.

The area around the neck hole is well-hidden, so it is more difficult to find head breakage or cracks in this area. Gently pull the head up to look at the neck. Sometimes the top rim of the head is covered with glue, and it is difficult to see cracks. Most dealers clean doll heads before selling them, so you should know if there are cracks in the neck area.

A few doll-repair people can repair a bisque head so perfectly it is difficult to detect repairs from the outside. These repairs must be made without firing. Close inspection will show a slight difference in the surface finish. The repainted surface is dull and lacks the glow of bisque.

Cracks—Auction catalogs and dealers' catalogs often list dolls as having a "hairline." A more accurate description of this is a "small, dark crack" or "a crack filled with dirt." You must see cracks to know how extensive they are and where they are located.

Never buy a doll with a crack on the face. It is preferable not to buy a doll if it has a crack anywhere on the head. If your economic circumstances dictate that you have a cracked head or no head at all, buy a doll with a *minor* crack.

Be careful because small cracks may be the beginning of something bigger. Look carefully. Some tiny cracks will not change and do not take away from the enjoyment of the doll.

Ears and Eyes—Another place on the head chips are often found is the ear lobe, where earrings of the wrong size were put in. The section around the eye can also be chipped.

A small chip in the ear lobe is not very important. It happens so often we are inclined to ignore it.

Chips around eyes *are* serious. When making a doll, porcelain is thinned or beveled around the eye to allow the glass eye to fit tightly. This procedure makes chipping more likely to occur. Chips around the eye take away from a doll's value. A doll with a chip or repair in the eye area is not pleasing to look at, and the chip decreases her beauty. To us, the eye area is one of the worst spots for damage.

Check to see if eyes have been replaced. If you find a French doll with blown or round glass eyes, they have been replaced. If you can see areas where the eye-setting plaster has been altered, assume eyes have been reset or replaced.

If a doll has a cracked eye, you probably won't find a replacement to match. Old paperweight eyes can sometimes be found, but they may not fit properly. Now, there are good, new paperweight eyes available for replacement even though beautiful old eyes are part of the doll's value.

Buying a Broken Doll—There are times when buying a broken doll is acceptable. For example, a very rare doll with a cracked head may be purchased by a museum. People come to the museum to see rare dolls, and a broken doll is better than no doll. There are instances when a collector will buy a broken doll because she wants one with a particular mark. She will replace the doll with a better one when it comes along. Some dolls are so rare another one may never come along.

ENTREPRENEURS OF FRENCH BÉBÉS

To be an entrepreneur, or to use your dolls to make money, you must become an expert on dolls. You must know and recognize many things about French dolls, such as modeling, painting, ear styles and costuming. You should be able to recognize different eyes, body shapes and joints. You must be able to identify markings and know where to look for them.

Left: A8T doll is 16 inches tall, and clothing is probably original. Cheeks are rosy. Large, almond-shaped eyes look deep and wet. Original mohair wig is thin. Doll has composition body.

It's wise to know the approximate price range of certain makes of dolls and to realize prices are constantly changing. Understand how much damage, and where, you can tolerate on a doll.

You must understand yourself—what you like and what will give you lasting joy. Do you want a doll that soothes you or stimulates you? Do you want a doll that is romantic, with simple serenity? Your desires will gradually and constantly change as you and your hobby mature together.

When you think you understand French dolls, know your desires and realize the limitations of your pocketbook, you will have the self-confidence to make your own selections. This is the point where you, as a collector, reach the height of enjoyment with your ability to use your dolls.

Many people use French Bébés as investments. Since the early 1970s, French dolls have been better than money in the bank. Many collectors use their dolls for profit. Some collectors use them for lectures or slide shows to entertain doll clubs and other interested groups.

Other collectors sell molds made from their old dolls for making reproduction dolls. Old dolls can be used to make and sell greenware or bisque heads. After a mold is made from an antique doll head, you can sell greenware, bisque heads or the mold itself.

Some people sell photographs of their dolls or post cards, posters and stationery made from photographs. Sometimes a museum is created with a collection. Other people copy original antique clothing, and sell entire costumes or patterns. One decorator we know decorates rooms, including the color scheme, around an antique doll. Some people sell dolls as a business, in addition to collecting them. But, as you can see, there are many ways to make a profit from French dolls without selling the actual doll.

Besides making a profit from dolls, there are other joys. You will make many friends—by mail and at sales, auctions and doll conventions when you are a collector.

You may be able to deduct all or part of your expenses for a trip if you conduct doll business on the trip. For example, it is considered business if you go to a doll show and have a sales table. You may be able to write off some of the cost of a doll on income taxes. An example of this is the purchase of a doll for the purpose of making a mold of its head. The doll is a deductible expense if you've set yourself up in that business.

You may also be able to use a part of your house as a deductible expense if work is done there on dolls. This could be a workshop or office used only for doll business. You may even be able to deduct a part of your utility bills. There are many hidden assets to being a doll collector and using dolls as a business. Be sure to check these out with your accountant or the Internal Revenue Service.

If you think you might want to use your dolls to make money, we have listed some points below that may help:
● Develop and use your own expertise for selecting dolls.
● Explore a collecting idea to its fullest.
● Be your own boss, and believe in your judgment.
● Develop or acquire the expertise you need, then use it.
● Use your natural talents.
● Identify any need in your collection and fill it.
● Seek new ways to collect.
● Find new ways to use your collection.
● Begin with the idea of succeeding.
● Don't be afraid to take risks when purchasing an unfamiliar doll. Fine collections of French dolls are not made without some risk and some mistakes.
● Get what you want. Go after it when you know what doll you want and where you're going.

There are times we abandon all guidelines we set for ourselves. Inflexible rules may blind us—sometimes we must place our faith alone in the beauty of a doll. At other times, we must meet a challenge head-on and buy a doll on the spur of the moment without research or total knowledge of its background.

JUDGE DOLLS INDIVIDUALLY

When buying French dolls, judge each doll on its own merit. Sometimes we become too anxious. When a doll is available with markings we want, we may buy it too quickly. Look at

Left: Incised *3H*, this doll is dressed in soft aqua satino covered with gossamer-thin silk Spanish lace. Shoes are unmarked, and she wears thick, old mohair wig.

each doll individually to be sure it's what you want. Be as selective as possible.

Look for Detail—Old molds were made and used as many as 50 times, and they wore down gradually with each pouring. Features on a doll poured first might be sharp and detailed, while the last 10 dolls might have soft features, without strong detail.

This happened with all doll heads made of porcelain and is obvious on many dolls. Comfort, one of our Bru dolls, has outstanding detail in her face. People fall in love with her when they see her.

Study facial features to see if details are strong. Expect to pay more for a doll with good facial features.

Ears are also an indication of how worn a mold was at the time of pouring. If ears are well-shaped and with detail, eyelids will probably still have a crease in them. Nostrils should be clean-cut and lips well-formed with a definite crease between them.

Molds that were reduced in size may lose detail. In some cases, the same face of one doll was made in many sizes. The SFBJ No. 236, called the *Laughing Jumeau*, is an example of a reduced head. (The doll is attributed to Jumeau, but it was made after Jumeau joined the SFBJ company.) The head was reduced from one for a 36-inch doll to a much smaller head for a 10-inch doll, with about 10 molds in between. In this process, some detail was lost in the reduction. Many people are aware of differences in the modeling of the two dolls but are unaware of how and why detail was lost.

Eyes—You must be able to recognize different kinds of eyes and what kind of eyes a French doll should have. Study eyes of different dolls, and see how they were made.

Be sure both eyes are the same size. It's good to know if eyes have been changed in a doll. Look inside the head, if possible. The color of old plaster ranges from dirty gray to white. Look at the edge of the plaster that now holds the eyes. If eyes have been changed, you will usually find extra bits of plaster or rings of dirt showing where the original plaster was.

Try to determine if the doll had sleep eyes. If there are pieces of cork glued inside the head (to stop the lead balance on the eyes), the doll probably had sleep eyes.

Study eyelashes. Only a few French dolls made after 1897 had hair eyelashes. Most French dolls had painted eyelashes. Paperweight eyes were handmade, so sometimes they do not fit exactly in the bisque opening. The eyes were set with a little wax around the edge to help fill in spaces and keep eyes in place. Wax also prevented plaster from leaking out onto the face when eyes were set.

When you look at a doll's face today, wax that has turned dark makes a dark rim just inside the bisque eye hole. This can add to the beauty of a doll. In some instances, wax is gone, which leaves a space around the eye, usually at the corners. This is often the case with eyes of antique Bru dolls. If a doll was stored face-up in a hot attic, wax often melted into the plaster.

When you look at a doll, it should look at you. We find dolls with improperly adjusted eyes can be hard to live with. If it is necessary to change eyes, you must realize it decreases the value of the doll.

Check eyelashes to see if they are well-painted. The art director of the Jumeau factory, Albert-Ernst Carrier-Belleuse, was a sculptor and painter. Other doll factories probably also had art directors. This would account for the perfection in the painting. Art directors taught and oversaw the painting of workers; the workers usually painted only one part of the doll, such as eyebrows, and turned out nearly perfect work.

Face Painting—Look at painting on the face. Some doll faces are painted better than others. Accent marks for lips sometimes miss the lips. In studying small French dolls, such as Milettes, we found this occurred several times.

Look at the cheek blush. Is there blush over the eyes? See page 119 for an explanation of other things to look for in face painting.

EXAMINING DOLLS

We feel you should first judge a doll from a distance. Think about her beauty and her appeal—this is most important when you judge a doll. Imagine it without wig and clothing.

Next, look more closely. Check the head for

Right: A11T in antique blue silk and gold silk lace. 27"

tiny brown marks which are metallic specks often found on old dolls. On the back of the head or on the neck, specks are of little consequence. But when they appear on the nose of a doll, like our Bru Jne 5 *Freckles*, they are important. See photo of Freckles on page 125.

We bought Freckles at an auction. She was in a glass case, above eye level. The catalog description said nothing about oxide specks on her nose. After we bought her, we discovered the brown spots on her face. We could have turned her back as a "faulty description," but Vernon looked at her and said, "I like her. Take her and let's call her Freckles." We did, but we hope you learn from our experience.

Examine the head for cracks or chips at the swivel neck or head rim. These may be covered. A reliable dealer will note these and call them to your attention. Tiny chips from ear lobes are also common. In our collecting, we do not consider these serious faults.

If the head doesn't please you, don't go any further with your study. You'll be wasting your time and the time of the doll's owner.

If you like the head, next check the wig. You should be able to tell if it's old or if it has been replaced. On Jumeau dolls, mohair wigs were used until 1896; then human-hair and mohair wigs were used. Other doll makers began using human-hair wigs about the same time.

Most modern wigs are marked on the nylon skullcap, over which the wig is made. This marking is as good as a label. We feel an old wig is better than a replacement wig, but a replacement is better than no wig.

When looking at the body, be more lenient. Some companies used papier-mâché bodies. Other doll makers added wood or sawdust to papier-mâché and called it *composition*. Most French doll makers used wood balls in joints, either glued to one joint or loose in the joint. Bodies were more apt to have part of the wood ball of the joint built in or glued into the lower leg or arm. Most doll makers used saucerlike

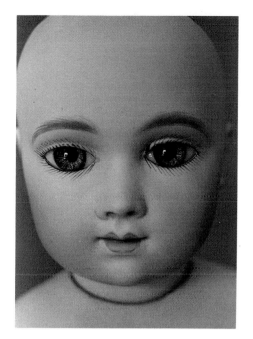

When selecting dolls, try to imagine doll without wig and clothes. Will she still be beautiful?

pieces of wood called *cuvets* in the joints for balls to move against. See photo on page 128.

Jumeau made what he called *unbreakable hands* of potassium silicate mixed with wood shavings and glue. If the original body is still on a Jumeau, its fingers are usually unbroken. Look for repaired hands. They can be ugly on a fine, well-costumed doll.

Check joints to be sure none are damaged. Expect to find some wear on bodies.

Judge clothing last. Clothing, especially original clothing, is important. Our book *Doll Costuming*, also by Scott Publications, can help you judge whether a costume is original. Be sure to see if shoes are marked.

We tell you what we've learned because as a connoisseur of fine dolls, you should know everything. But don't expect perfection in antique French dolls that were once toys.

Left: Mint-condition doll, incised *Bru Jne 7*, is 18 inches tall. Matched underclothing, socks, shoes, dress and wig are original.

Doll Companies
of France

French doll-making companies that made the childlike Bébé were located in and around Paris. They all competed for the same trade.

Companies were constantly experimenting with new inventions, new products and new ideas to increase the sale of their dolls. They did not hesitate to "borrow" ideas from other factories. Among the things they experimented with were eye movements, walking movements and voice boxes. Only a few experimental dolls have survived until today, and a one-of-a-kind doll or a doll made in a small production run is an excellent collector's doll.

There is still much that is unknown about the manufacture of dolls 100 years ago. Some companies assembled heads and bodies. Some had the heads made by another company and marked with their own initials. Some companies bought whiteware, which was fired porcelain.

Owning kilns, developing porcelain and the actual job of modeling and producing heads was difficult. Consequently, there were problems and many small companies were bought or taken over by larger ones. This is indicated by the words "controlled by" in a company's name. For example, with Danel and Co. dolls, we find in company descriptions, "Danel and Co., controlled by Jumeau."

Dolls from the same company were made in different qualities, even from the same design. There were dramatic differences in the bisque and painting within the same company.

Some doll making companies survived many years and made dolls under the leadership of several directors. Often this change left its mark on the dolls. A good collector can spot the differences in older and newer dolls by looking closely at eyebrow decoration, lip painting or the type of eyes used.

We provide this overview of French doll-making companies to help you in your comparison of different dolls. We won't spend a lot of time on dates and unimportant details. We do include important identification items to help you.

MOTHEREAU

Alexandra Celestin Triburee Mothereau made Bébés for about 15 years, from 1880 to 1895. He could not have made very many dolls because they are so very scarce. Few collectors have them. They seem to vary in quality of bisque and type of body. Mothereaux are marked with a number and B.M.

Early Depose Jumeau, incised, 21". Wig is mohair, dress is blue silk.

Mothereau doll marked 7 BM. 19"

P10G. Pintel and Godchaux. 19"

P.G. BÉBÉ

Dolls marked with *P.G.* and a size number, were thought to be those of Paul Girard of the House of Bru. They were often sold as Brus.

Now a doll, box, and label has been found proving the dolls marked P.G. belonged to the production of Henri Pintel and Ernest Godchaux. They made dolls from 1887 to 1899 when they joined SFBJ.

H-DOLLS

We now know that Aristide M. Halopeau was the maker of the doll incised with the block H and size number. Heads are extremely scarce. The dolls are exceptionally beautiful, and heads and bodies are the highest quality. These dolls are a collector's dream.

We have tracked down the sizes that are known to collectors. Size 0 is 16 inches, size 1 is 18 inches, size 2 is 20 inches, size 3 is 22 inches

and size 4 is 24 inches. There may be larger sizes, but it is doubtful there is a size below 0.

Markings on the heads are located in exactly the same place on each doll and done in the same block letters. Sometimes the mark is lightly impressed, and other times it is impressed deeply. The size number comes first, followed by the letter *H*.

Learn from Dolls—We have determined certain things about H-dolls from the dolls themselves. The doll-making company was in existence before 1890 because all the heads we have examined are pressed, not poured, porcelain. See page 114 for an explanation of pressed and poured heads. After 1890, almost all doll-making companies poured porcelain in molds. The quality of

Right: P13G. Made by Pintel and Godchaux. 25"

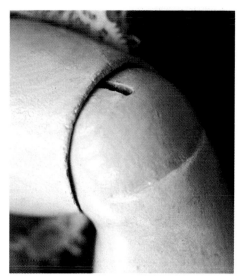

Well-formed, smooth-working knee joint of H-doll.

1H-doll has a pressed head and applied, pierced ears. She has wood body and wears her original costume.

bisque, the fine paperweight eyes and the beautiful craftmanship of the wood bodies indicate these dolls were made at the height of the doll-making era. Even the use of luxurious angora wigs indicates the company intended to make a superior product.

Bodies on H-dolls are the best crafted we have found on French dolls. All body parts are wood, and there are no extra balls or pieces. Everything fits well and works smoothly, as if it were oiled. Slits in wood for joints are very narrow. Fingers are separated and posed in a graceful position. Feet and toes are well-carved on the top *and* bottom of the foot, and an arch is carved in. The calf of the leg is a little heavy.

Other Dolls with H Markings—We are often contacted about dolls with H markings. Most turn out to be dolls other than the elusive French H-doll. June Lillibridge, of Strasburg, Ohio, sent me one of her dolls, which was incised *13H* in the middle of the head. After examination, we concluded the doll was German and probably made by Handwerck or Hamburger & Co. The doll had sleep eyes and an open mouth with teeth.

We have seen at least two lady fashion dolls with an *H* on the head or shoulderplate. One mold maker advertised an H-doll mold, but after examining it, it appears to be a mold of a German doll.

Face painting of H-1 doll is delicate. Blue of costume enhances beautiful blue eyes.

Left: Incised 4H-doll, 24". Extra long mohair wig was used only on expensive dolls. Her smooth-working wood body is well finished. We believe shoes, dress, and underclothing are original.

Identifying H-dolls — Use caution and do some detective work before you spend a huge sum for a marked H-doll. Before you spend your money, be sure you are buying the French masterpiece.

Study the shape of the face—the face of an H-doll is rather square. Eyes are paperweight, sometimes with threading. (*Threading* is tiny rays in the iris of an eye, made with glass threads.) Painting is perfect.

The head was pressed, not poured, and ears were applied. The *H* and number are incised just under the rim of the head. Study the photo of the H-doll marking on page 161 that we have included to help you identify an H-doll.

HOUSE OF BRU

We must speak of the "House of Bru" because all the dolls had the Bru name long after the business was run by people other than a Bru.

During 1991 there was a tremendous amount of research done on Bru by Francois Theimer and Florence Theriault. A bit of information we had found earlier is now considered invalid.

Bru dolls, both fashion and lady, were assembled by Leon Casimir Bru and his wife Appolyne on St. Denis Street in Paris. The heads were made by Barrois. Leon Casimir Bru had worked for a doll assembler for a short time before deciding to start his own business. Appolyne, a seamstress, provided the elaborate costumes for the lovely fashion dolls, which were unmarked except for the letters on the head. Later lady dolls were marked B. Jne et Cie, B.J. or R.B. (Barrois).

In 1883 the Bru business was sold to Henri Chevrot, who produced all the wonderful designs of Bru Jne. The last owner of the Bru Company, Paul Girard, took over in 1890.

In a study of the faces used on the wonderful Bru Bébé we find really only three shapes from three master molds.

The earliest of the children dolls was the unmarked Breveté. For identification, it had only the sticker on the chest. This doll had cupped-like hands with each nail outlined in pink. The head was mounted on a shoulder-plate and placed on a leather body.

All of the other French companies placed their first Bébé heads on composition bodies. Leon Casimir Bru had been producing leather bodies

Incised *Bru Jne 11* is 27 inches tall. She has soft, innocent look—all Brus look as if they were made by the same sculptor.

Bru Jne 9, leather body and feet. 25"

Left: 4H-doll has fine, smooth bisque and deep blue eyes. Her brows are softly feathered. Lips are slightly parted, with deeper color between them.

18" Bru Jne 7 with leather body and feet.

This 15-1/2 inch doll is incised with circle and dot and *Size 3*. She has exceptionally nice, deep-blue paperweight eyes. We know doll was made by Bru, even though she is not marked Bru.

for lady dolls so he made a leather body in child-like proportions for the Bébés.

In between each change of production of Brus, there were always transition dolls, made during the change-over. These dolls had parts of both new and old productions.

We present a transition doll, Bru Jne 5, 17'' tall (*Left*). She has the face of the Breveté and a leather body that resembles parts of the Breveté and the Bru Jne. This doll has the lovely ballerina hands of the new Bru Jne. Today, these Breveté dolls are popular and add to any Bru collection. (See Brevetés *page 2.*)

Other transition Brus between the Breveté and the Bru Jne are the Circle-and-Dot Bru or the Crescent Bru, which came after the Breveté. This was an entirely new face — the second master mold of Bébé Brus.

Breveté Bru
Jne transition
Bru Jne 5, 17''

Right: Bru Jne 15, 36'' on a Bru composition body.

Bru Jne 5, 15'' wood legs (not all 5's are the same size or look alike).

Bru Jne 5 is 16'' and has wood legs, Chevrot body.

Bru Jne 3, 15'' Chevrot body

With its heavy baby-like cheeks and teeth (yes, teeth!), this face was modified slightly once during production. The Circle-and-Dot and Crescent Brus all came from the same master mold.

Leon Casimir Bru had sculpted the Bébé Bru Jne and the master mold was made before Chevrot bought the business. This was Bru Bébé master mold number three, which produced a successful business for Chevrot for seven years. Bébé Bru Jne was modeled to be a child, older than the Circle Dot Bru.

Hundreds of different Bru faces were conceived from this master Bru Jne mold. Actually, all Bru Jne faces are taken from this same mold. The differences, and there were many, were made by cutting the eyes larger or smaller, and by the removal of the teeth or tongue line. The basic shape was left untouched.

Other subtle differences were made in the painting, the shape of the brows, and the shape of the lips. Even the color of the eyes changed the Bru so that while one was spectacular, another was mediocre.

Henri Chevrot added a new body for the Bru Jne head. Usually, we refer to this body, with its slimmed down tummy and hips, as the "Chevrot Bru body." He added a pin joint at the elbow and another at the knee, and made the lower legs of

Bru dolls with leather bodies. Bru Jne 7, on right, is older. Note slim waist and hips of Bru Jne 5 on left. Dolls have pin-jointed arms.

Leather bodied Bru Jne 12 is 31''. She wears Bru dress in blue to match her eyes.

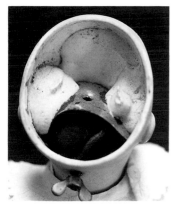

Inside of Nursing Bru head showing original mechanism.

Nursing Bru 13", Bru Jne 1 in all original clothing.

wood. The lower arms were bisque, with a few exceptions of wood.

Overlapping the Bru Jne on the Chovrot body was the "Nursing Bru," the most popular Bru doll ever produced. It sold and kept selling, even after SFBJ took over production in 1899. Mouths on the Bru Jne heads were remodeled to become the "Nursing Brus." The mechanism (photo) was added in the head for drawing water from a bottle.

There was also an "Eating Bru," which is seldom seen. Dry food was put into the mouth of "Bébé Germond." The food fell down through the body and came out the foot. Shoes were made

Reproduction Bru Jne 5 in antique Polish skating outfit. A good reproduction Bru is okay if you can't have the antique!

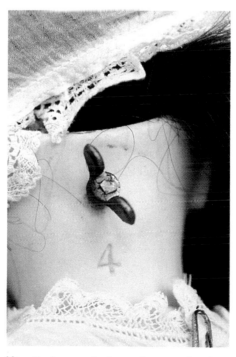

Key that operated nursing mechanism on back of head of Nursing Bru. Similar key on back of Jumeau head opened and closed eyes.

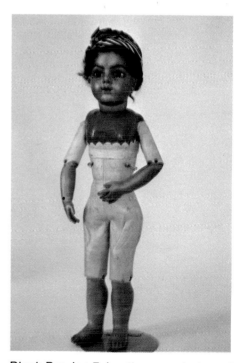

Black Bru Jne 7. Leather was darkened but is not as dark as arms and legs. Feet are wood, and arms are bisque. Arms and legs have pin joints.

Left: Incised *Bru Jne 4*, doll wears original dress and hat. Brown paperweight eyes do not look as deep as blue eyes on Brus.

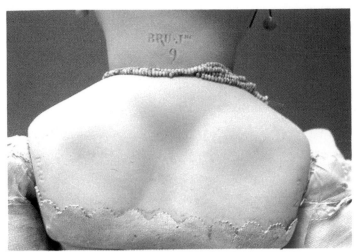

Back view of shoulderplate of Bru shows how it was carefully and realistically modeled. Note Bru mark on neck.

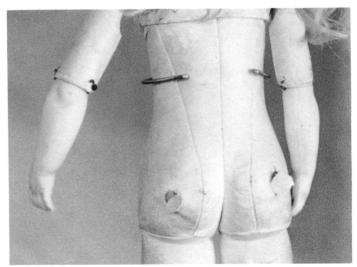

Leather bodies can be straightened by removing some filling.

Leather body and legs, 23" Bru Jne 8

with little flaps to take out the food. "Bébé Germond" had heavy, very chubby bisque legs that were not used on any other Bru.

The same hand molds were used repeatedly. The first hand, with the curved-under fingers on the Breveté was used only on the Brevetés. The ballerina hand was and is the loveliest and most artistic of any hands made by any company of that time. The hands were used first on short arms that went into a leather sleeve, then used as well as the pin-jointed, elbow length arms. Apparently, these forearms were not sized down with every head reduction, but were used in one size for all three head sizes.

Other Bru hands were made of wood and none of those were shaped like the ballerina hands.

Very early in the Bru production, composition bodies were made, but they were neither many nor popular. Today, many people think that all com-

position Bru bodies were a late production, but upon checking, we find it was started by Bru Jne. Then, after 1890, Brus were again made with composition bodies by Paul Girard.

One of the most wonderful Brus ever made was the Bru Jne 7 that had an all-wood body. In 1869, Leon Casimir Bru Jne, advertised his lady dolls on all-wood bodies, jointed at the waist, ankles and wrists, as well as at the shoulders, hips, and elbows. About 10 years later, Bru Jne copied the wood body for a Bébé, changing the lady-type wood body to childlike proportions for the doll named "Bébé Modèle."

That body construction was absolutely wonderful for posing a doll. With all the joints the original lady dolls had (except the waist), the dolls could be posed in any position. That wood body proved too expensive and time consuming to make, so few were produced.

Apparently the wood body was not made at all during the time of Chevrot. Some eight years later, Chevrot produced a modified version of the wood body with joints, more or less as we see in composition bodies.

During the time of Chevrot, the Brus that we know and love were produced with the finest

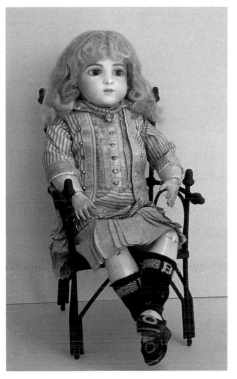

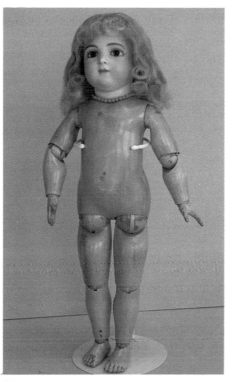

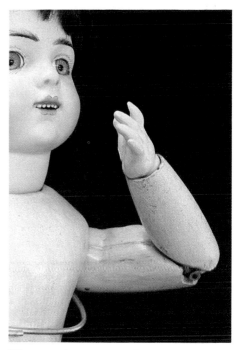

Bru´Jne 7 on all-wood body with multiple joints.

The wood body by Casimir Bru Jr. Bru Jne 7

When string is pulled, arm comes up and throws a kiss. Doll also has crying voice.

craftsmanship. These are the Bru Jnes that stand in our cases and represent the ultimate in dollmaking.

In 1889, the House of Bru changed hands again when Paul Girard took over. Girard altered the Bru Jnes from the old master mold to a look that was barely recognizable. And, he added an "R" to the signature. Girard made teeth, and open mouths, and altered the chin. He made kiss-throwing Brus, walking Brus, and added in other of his inventions.

NOTE: There were other patents and inventions from the time Bru began his doll business, but the main ones that collectors' treasure have been mentioned here.

This list shows the sequence of Bru bodies, which, of course, overlapped in production:
1. Leather and wood lady bodies
2. Breveté chubby leather body, leather feet, half bisque arms
3. Circle and Dot chubby leather body, leather feet, half bisque arms
4. All-wood multi-jointed body, wood hands and feet
5. Gusseted leather body, leather lower legs, elbow length bisque arms
6. Slim leather body (Chevrot), pin-jointed wood lower legs, pin-jointed bisque arms
7. Same body with wood pin-jointed lower arms
8. Wood body with eight joints
9. Composition body
10. Kiss-throwing composition body

FLEISCHMANN & BLÖDEL

The Fleischmann & Blödel Co. was originally located in Bavaria but established a branch in Paris. They produced dolls from 1873 to 1914. The company was one of the original members of the SFBJ. See page 82 for more on SFBJ.

In 1890, the company began making the Eden Bébé (see page 46). The doll has a Bru-shaped face, but painting is so crude you probably wouldn't notice the similarity. Lips are brighter red than most dolls of this period. Lashes and brows are strongly painted, harsh and glossy.

The company worked on new inventions and registered patents for movements in many dolls, including walking, turning the head, moving eyelids and kissing-and-walking mechanisms.

ÉTIENNE DENAMUR

Étienne Denamur made dolls of fine bisque in Paris from 1857 to 1898. Dolls marked E.D. could have been made by Denamur. The company registered several patents and advertised its dolls had the "best articulated" composition bodies. Very little is known about the company. We do not even know for certain if dolls marked

Incised Block F3G. 20". Note how chubby this face is.

E14D Depose. 28" has smooth, perfect bisque.

Incised E I D. 14"

E.D. are by Étienne Denamur—E. Dumont and E. Daspres had the same initials.

Dolls marked *E.D.* usually have teeth and open, pleasant, smiling mouths. The company also made some dolls with closed mouths.

EDMOND DASPRES

Another doll-making company with the initials *E.D.* made dolls from 1902 to 1908. The company was owned by Edmond Daspres. Daspres was the director who succeeded Jules Steiner in the Steiner Co. in 1906. Two trademarks, *LeParisien* and *LaPatricienne*, were registered by Daspres. Steiner dolls with these marks were made *before* Daspres took over from Steiner but were not registered.

We found a papier-mâché body in a crude lady shape with the initials EDB and the words *LaPatricienne* stamped on her hip. What was unusual about the doll was the head was marked *A9T*, and it had an open mouth and many small teeth. This is part of the fun of doll collecting — finding new things and discovering new markings (page 53)!

Right: E.D. doll with open mouth and teeth is 22 inches tall. Bisque is fine-textured, and doll is well-painted. She seems to be smiling.

DANEL AND CO.

From 1889 to 1895, Danel and Co. made dolls in Paris. Dolls of this company are well-marked. The head is incised, and the body is stamped with a picture of the Eiffel Tower.

We usually find two dolls credited to Danel. The Paris Bébé was made to celebrate the completion of the Eiffel Tower and the company also made Bébé Française (see page 18). Danel was the first company to specialize in black and mulatto dolls. The dolls we have seen are very attractive.

In 1890, the company changed from stringing dolls with elastic to using metal springs. Springs were supposed to last forever without stretching. We have a Paris Bébé strung completely with springs, and she is as tight today as when she was made. By 1896, Jumeau had gained control of the company.

RABERY AND DELPHIEU

Rabery and Delphieu produced dolls in Paris from 1856 to 1898. Most R.D. dolls are attractive, well-made Bébés that range from the No. 1, which is 14 inches tall, to the No. 4, which is 23 inches tall. These dolls have smooth, fine, light-colored bisque and blue or brown paperweight eyes.

Rabery and Delphieu's successor, Gentry, experimented with walking dolls, talking dolls, sleeping dolls and kiss-throwing dolls. R.D. dolls are found in many collections.

PETIT AND DUMONTIER

Dolls were made in Paris by Petit and Dumontier from 1878 to 1890. Not many dolls are found with the *P.D.* mark on their heads. For many years, we have assumed these dolls were made by Petit and Dumontier. To date, we have no reason to doubt this, although it has not yet been proved.

P.D. dolls can be recognized by the close positioning of their eyes. They have pleasant-looking faces and appear to have been made by the same sculptor.

We have only two P.D. dolls in our collection. Our dolls, and apparently all other P.D. dolls on original bodies, have metal hands with an articulated joint at the wrist. Arms and legs seem too long in proportion to the head. These dolls have fine paperweight eyes and cork pates.

Left: Incised *R4D*, doll is 23 inches tall and wears old, human hair wig. She is in good condition because she was in a museum for 40 years. Her original black-and-gray taffeta costume is still lovely.

Little French dolls are also called *Milettes.* Clockwise, from left to right: Schmitt; F.G.; E.J.; A.T.; E.D.; Incised Jumeau.

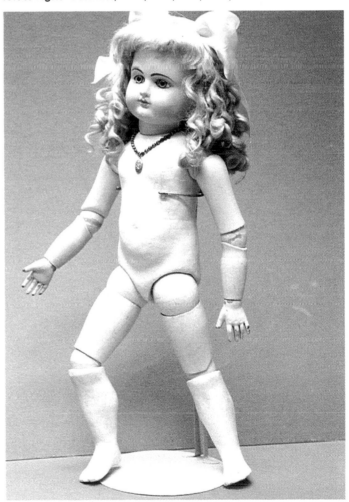

Petit and Dumontier body was long and gangly, made of wood and composition. Hands are metal.

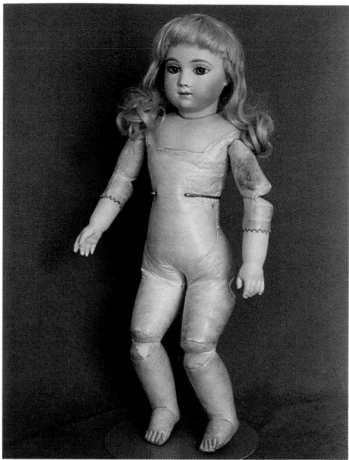

Early A.T.s had leather bodies and beautifully modeled bisque hands. Bodies were stuffed with bran.

Incised *A7T* is appealing Snow Angel. She is 18 inches tall and has leather body and bisque hands.

ANDRE JEAN THUILLIER

Andre Jean Thuillier produced the Bébés in the 1880s. A.T. dolls are among the most desired dolls. Their charm and beautiful eyes make them very appealing. A.T. dolls are made of fine bisque and are usually well decorated. Some dolls have more intense coloring than others. A few later A.T.s have two rows of tiny teeth. Bisque is not as good on late dolls, and painting is a little sloppy.

Early A.T. dolls are the ones collectors desire. It is obvious by the workmanship that later A.T.s may have been made by another company but from Thuillier's molds.

Most A.T.s were produced by the older method of pressing porcelain in the mold. All A.T. dolls have finely applied ears, and ears are pierced through the lobe.

Some faces of A.T.s have more detail in the modeling than others because molds wore down. They appear to have been originally modeled by the same artist.

A.T. Bodies—The finest A.T. dolls seem to have white-leather, gusseted bodies similar to early Bru bodies. The leather is pinked (point cut into it like pinking shears) around the shoulderplate. Feet are leather, with sewn-in toes.

We opened one A.T. body to straighten it. Inside we found it stuffed with grain chaff, not sawdust or cork. See photo on page 53.

On leather bodies, we have found three different bisque hands. All hands were attached by inserting the lower arm into leather at the midway point of the forearm. The loveliest hands are found on an A7T. Hands have separate fingers and tinted cuticles. The hand is in a relaxed position similar to, but unlike, the Bru bisque hand.

Another hand on an A3T has fingers modeled at a sharp angle, as if they were meant to hold something. One A.T. doll, owned by our daughter Colleen, has a more relaxed, babylike hand.

Other A.T.s have well-made wood bodies. These bodies are smooth working, without balls in the joints. Wood hands are rather flat. Bodies are unmarked, and they do not match other bodies we have.

Later A.T. dolls, with open mouths and teeth, are found on an unusual assortment of crude

Right: Doll incised *A9T* is 20 inches tall. She wears her original dress and has matching bonnet of pale green decorator satin.

bodies. We think something drastic happened to cause the change. The company may have changed hands or formulas may have been lost.

Some examples are composition bodies with jointed-at-the-wrist hands. There are large bodies, such as the 28-inch A.T. doll we once owned with a molded bosom and little other shaping. There is a lady body with a wasplike waist, large bosom and crude joints. See photo at right.

We have one example of an A9T head on a strange body marked *EDB* and *LaPatricienne*. As noted on page 46, this mark was registered to Edmond Daspres, who succeeded Steiner in the Steiner Co. in 1906. Before we jump to conclusions that Steiner or Daspres took over Thuillier's doll works, we must mention a Simon and Halbig head that was found on a similar body with the same markings. Doll heads were moved from body to body, as they are today. Perhaps Daspres or Steiner supplied the bodies to someone using Thuillier molds. Later A.T. bodies seem to be light papier-mâché, painted ivory, instead of heavier composition used by Thuillier.

There is little historical information available on A.T. dolls. At first, we reversed the dates of the bodies. We thought crude bodies were produced earlier. But after studying the dolls, we have determined they were made in the following order:

1. Fine leather bodies, with beautiful heads and bisque hands.
2. Good, sturdy wood bodies with excellent heads.
3. Heads with open mouths and run-of-the-mill composition of papier-mâché bodies.

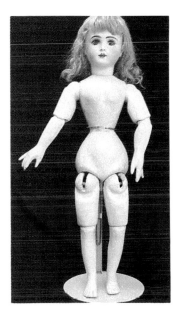

A.T.s were made in a range of sizes, from the No. 2 at 12-1/2 inches to the No. 15 at 32 inches. There are also numbers that do not fit any scale. Numbers may indicate the type of body used.

Crude papier-mâché body in lady-like shape with A9T head. This is a rare, unusual body.

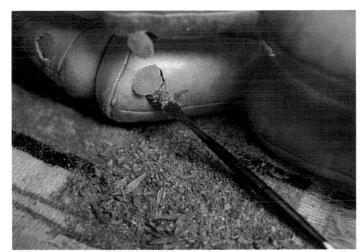

It was surprising to find A.T. bodies filled with chaff and bran, not cork.

Andre Jean Thuilliers. 15''. A.T. in all-original clothes.

Left: A8T doll is 16 inches tall. Cheeks are highly blushed, and brows and lips are softly painted. She wears original clothing and old mohair wig.

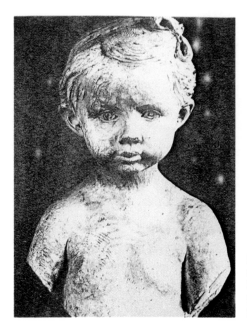
Photo of terra cotta sculpture by A. Marque has same features as Albert Marque dolls.

ALBERT MARQUE

Albert Marque dolls are the rarest, most-expensive, most-coveted dolls in the world. Their prices hovered around $30,000 for many years. Then, in 1983, one sold at auction for the incredible price of $38,000. Anyone who has owned a Marque will agree the dolls may be worth the high price. Now in 1992, they range from $100,000 to $120,000.

Marque dolls are exquisite and seem to "grow on you." They are more than playthings, more than heirlooms—they are objects of art.

When we purchased our pair of Marque dolls, they were a mystery, and few people were aware of them. The dolls were signed *A. Marque*, and not even the first name of the doll maker was known.

We studied the details of the head. Vernon, who is a mold maker, noted there were five pieces to the head mold, so we know the artist was not an ordinary doll maker. Doll makers made heads in two pieces for easy production.

With the help of librarians, we began research on French sculptors. We consulted the *Dictionnaire des Peintres Sculpteurs, Dessinateurs et Graveurs*, (Dictionary of Painters, Sculptures, Designers and Engravers) by Benezit, and found some information on Marque. We discovered the "A" stood for Albert, and he was born in France in 1872. The book listed some of his awards and sculptures. He was called the "friend of small children" because he made many sculptures of children's heads. In 1980, we

discovered Marque's obituary in the June 16, 1939, edition of *Beaux Arts*.

Once the initial step was made, we began to find other information on Marque's work. We searched for a date for the dolls because Marque was active for a very long time.

In the UFDC's 1976 convention book, there is a picture of a Marque doll owned by Laddie Fuller. The doll had been won in a Paris raffle by Laddie's aunt during World War I. At first we thought this might be our only source for dating Marque dolls.

Another long-time owner of a Marque doll says her doll came wrapped in a 1914 Paris newspaper. A third date we found was the April 13, 1916, importation date of the Carnegie Museum. The museum imported six Marques; they still have five dolls. All these dates help us pinpoint when Marque dolls were made.

We researched the travels of *our* Marque dolls. They were originally purchased in the late 1930s or early '40s by Gaynell Denson from Harriet Miller. Miller owned an antique shop specializing in French dolls, and she located 10 or 12 Marque dolls in a warehouse in Canada. We assume most of the Marque dolls in the United States came from her because we have found no other source for the dolls. When Miller sold the Marques to collectors in the '30s, she sold them in pairs for $300 each. As we recalled in the section beginning on page 6, we found our Marques in a closed museum owned by Gaynell Denson.

We now have a more-exact date for the making of Marque dolls. The sculpture of a young girl (a bust in terra cotta), shown above left, owned by a couple in California has *exactly* the same features as the well-known Marque doll. The bust is signed *A. Marque* and dated 1913. We feel certain Marque dolls were made the same time as the sculpture because the dolls are a reproduction of the bust.

The Sculpting of Marque Dolls—In addition to the five-piece head mold, there are other interesting things about the sculpting and construction of the Marque dolls. The top of a Marque head is cut level, not on a slant as other French dolls. The body was made only for this doll and has unusual side-jointed hips with an attached

Right: This 18-inch doll by unknown maker is sometimes sold as a Marque, but it is not. Neither modeling nor workmanship resemble Marque dolls.

ball in the joint. Legs are long and slender. Arms below the elbow are bisque, and hands were modeled with the same skill as the head.

The sculpture of the face of a Marque doll is different from other dolls. Features are sharp, elfin and well-defined. Ears protrude like a real child's. The forehead curve is minimized on French dolls, but this is not true of Marque dolls.

When Marque dolls were created, most doll makers were making open mouths and sleep eyes. The Marque has blue or brown paperweight eyes and a closed mouth.

All Marque dolls are 22 inches tall. All the dolls were made from the same mold and have the same body.

Costumes of Marque Dolls—We assume Marque dolls were made for the shop of Mme. Margaine Lacroix in Paris because *all* Marque dolls in original costume bear her label. The dolls from the Carnegie Museum were purchased from Lacroix, and the Miller dolls came to Canada from Lacroix. Mme. Lacroix was an accomplished costumer and an authority on historical French costumes.

Dolls were dressed in the finest fabrics, and the costumes are rich and elaborate. Clothes were made of silk, velvet, silk taffeta and other fabrics. The most beautiful fabrics and trims were used, whether Lacroix was costuming queens (we have a record of five queens at the Carnegie Museum) or peasants, such as the doll in the Margaret Strong Museum in Rochester, New York.

Because Marque dolls are scarce and expensive, you might wonder why we devote so much of our time to them. Through our books, we present many different types of rare dolls for readers to study, even though people may not be able to collect them. We want you to know the faces of different dolls and be able to recognize them if you should find one. We *know* there are undiscovered Marques around. We also want you to recognize a reproduction Marque—a reproduction doll is *always* smaller.

The following story is an example of finding one of these rare dolls. On September 4, 1984, Alvina Kincaid of Milwaukie, Oregon, called us to say she was repairing a marked Albert Marque doll! She was shocked when the owner, Barbara Treyne,

brought the doll in to be repaired for her granddaughter.

Alvina is 80 years old and has been repairing dolls for many years, but she had never seen a Marque doll. Because she had seen pictures of our Marque dolls in our books, Alvina recognized this doll as the genuine Marque that it was. She was also aware of the doll's rarity and value.

The doll had been purchased in France in 1918 and brought back as a present to Barbara when she was 5. She played with the blue-eyed doll for many years, which accounts for the loss of one arm and all of its clothing. The doll was originally dressed in a flowered skirt, black bolero jacket, white blouse and straw hat. She still wears her original blond wig.

If you find a Marque doll, as did Alvina, contact us through Scott Publications. You'll be helping us to continue our research on this rare, beautiful doll.

MAISON (HOUSE OF) JUMEAU

The Jumeau Co. began making dolls in Paris in 1842 and continued until 1938. These dolls are

Doll marked *Déposé Tête Jumeau* is 13 inches tall and wears original clothing, shoes and wig. Jumeau did not use human-hair wigs until late 1890s, so this doll had to be made after that time.

Left: Déposé Tête Jumeau is 17 inches tall. Note well-painted brows and generous lashes. This type of doll is often the first French doll added to a collection.

Long-Faced Jumeau is 32 inches tall. She wears a child's old white dress.

Showing metal spring in head — original stringing of Jumeaus.

probably the most-loved, most-collected French dolls available to collectors. There is not as much variation among Jumeau dolls as there was with other doll makers, but almost all Jumeaus are beautiful.

Identifying Jumeaus—It's sometimes easier for a collector to recognize and identify Jumeau Bébés if dolls are divided into groups. We divide them by age and marks, and prices of dolls should reflect this.

1. Premier (very early) unmarked Bébés, or *Portrait dolls*, including the Long-Faced Jumeau, are the oldest Jumeaus. These have exceptionally fine eyes, and some eyes are threaded. We consider the Long-Faced Jumeau important to collectors and deal with her separately, beginning on page 61.

2. The *Incised Jumeau*, incised Déposé Jumeau, or a rare doll with *Jumeau* in a frame, are the second-oldest dolls. They are light bisque but often have eye holes cut of different sizes and poorly fitted paperweight eyes.

3. Dolls marked *E.J.* with the size number are the third oldest. These dolls always seem to be high-quality, with good eyes and good wigs.

4. Dolls stamped in red with *Déposé Tête Jumeau Bte SGDG* on the back of the neck are the next group.

5. Dolls stamped in red with only *Tête Jumeau* are often found with an open mouth and teeth.

Early bodies of Jumeau dolls had eight ball-joints and straight wrists. These bodies were usually stamped in blue. The next body made by Jumeau had four ball-joints and straight wrists. Later, a joint was added to the wrist to give more articulation and movement, and all the balls at joints were fastened to arms or legs.

Stringing Bodies and Attaching Heads—Jumeau bodies were strung in a particular way. We describe it here so you can look at a Jumeau and tell if it has been restrung. If you have a Jumeau, look into the head of the doll as you read the following description.

Heads were attached with a 1½ inch spring, with a wood washer at each end of the spring. A wire went down through the spring. The bottom hook on the wire went over the bar in the middle of the body. To hook the wire, a person pushed (with a thumb) on the bent-over top of the wire in the head. It was a quick, easy method that never loosened. Legs were strung over the same bar of wood across the middle of the body. Early Jumeau dolls had a wood bar glued across the body during assembly.

Right: Long-Faced Jumeau with no marks except *13*. Brows are dark and narrow, and ears are pierced.

Creating Jumeau Dolls—In our research, we found references to Mlle. Delphine Floss as the creator of some molds for Jumeau. But additional research attributes most of the creation of molds to Albert-Ernst Carrier-Belleuse, the sculptor of the Long-Faced Jumeau.

Most heads by Jumeau are incised or stamped. A few of the early dolls (Portrait Jumeaus) and dolls made in 1890s (dolls sold unmarked at a lower price) were not marked *Jumeau*. These later heads were often marked with check marks or tick marks, which were sometimes red or sometimes black. Marks included initials, strokes and numbers. Heads with only tick marks are usually credited to Jumeau. See the section on markings beginning on page 154.

Jumeau is credited with many inventions and novelty dolls, including walking, talking and eye movements. The company didn't hesitate to use novel ideas of other doll makers. It claimed the swivel-head invention, but it was patented by Huret. After the introduction of a phonograph doll, made by Edison and a German doll-making company, Jumeau decided to make one. The Jumeau company kept up with different changes, adding dolls with open mouths and teeth as soon as they became popular.

Long-Faced Jumeau—This Jumeau doll is called the *Long-Faced Jumeau, Jumeau Triste, Sad-Faced Jumeau, Cody Jumeau* or *Portrait Jumeau*. Long-Faced Jumeaus are popular all over the world and are called by many names. However they all refer to the same doll. Whatever she's called, this is an important doll to collectors because of her unusual charm.

This early doll, with pale bisque and large eyes, intrigues many collectors. From the moment we set eyes on her unusual, appealing face, we wanted to own one. These dolls often seem to hold even more allure for men who collect dolls.

Recent research leads us to believe this doll is an important part of doll history—she was the first Bébé. There seems to be no doubt that the sculptor who created it was Albert-Ernst Carrier-Belleuse. He was also the titled sculptor for Napoleon III for many years.

Many researchers believe King Henry IV, as a child of 4, was the inspiration for the sculpture

Jumeau wears original wig, which adds to her value. Wigs were usually the first to deteriorate when doll was played with.

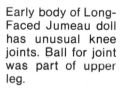

Early body of Long-Faced Jumeau doll has unusual knee joints. Ball for joint was part of upper leg.

19-inch Jumeau is unmarked except for red or black check marks and tick marks. Dolls with these marks are attributed to Jumeau.

Left: Premier Jumeau. 14". In all original clothing. Marked 3.

E.J. 8. 18". Nice even-toned dark skinned Jumeau, (full view page 3).

A perfect E J 9 in original costume.

of the Long-Faced Jumeau, and a painting of the future king was used to create the model. In comparing the painting with the doll, there are strong similarities. Many of us, in trying to create a term for older Jumeau dolls, have called them *Portrait Jumeaus*. It seems we were right all along.

These dolls were made over a period of years. Early dolls have characteristics that are more desired by collectors. Differences are subtle, but study shows the older, first-made Long-Faced Jumeau was very pale bisque. Face painting was also delicate, and the head and body were of superb quality.

In the first version of the Long-Faced Jumeau, the deep-blue paperweight eyes are slightly off-center—the pupil is set toward the top. There is mauve blushing above eyes. Ears are applied. The body is ball-jointed, with straight wrists, and fingers are separated. The ball from the

Left: E.J.6 is 18 inches tall, and E2J is 11 inches tall. E.J. dolls, made by Émile Jumeau, are beautiful and bring higher prices than stamped Tête Jumeaus.

Attractive French doll, marked with black *HI* in china paint. This is *not* the coveted, sought-after incised H-doll but may be a Portrait Jumeau. Doll has *9* incised on neck. Other marks may be tick marks.

Doll marked only with a *9* has Jumeau-marked body. Shape of face tells you it is a Long-Faced Jumeau. She is 20 inches tall.

knee is attached to the upper leg—we haven't seen this on any other doll. The body is stamped *Jumeau*, and the head has only a size number. Numbers on the neck are slightly off-center.

The second version varies slightly. Cheek and lip color are a little deeper, and eyes are centered. The body is a later type with ball-joints. All these dolls are so lovely that few collectors would be picky enough to quibble about a slight color variation of face painting.

Long-Faced Jumeaus were made in sizes from 6 to 16. There is a story there was also a size 20 model in the studio of Carrier-Belleuse, but we have no evidence it was ever produced.

The method of first modeling the head in clay, then making a plaster mold was used with this doll. For further information on sculpting doll heads, see page 109. The sculpted head was then cast in *hydrocal,* which is a very hard plaster. Refinement was done on the plaster model. A visitor to the studio of Carrier-Belleuse wrote about seeing a plaster model of the Long-Faced Jumeau.

There are stories that the granddaughter of Carrier-Belleuse was the model for the Long-Faced Jumeau. The great-granddaughter of Carrier-Belleuse, Mme. Triana, said in an interview that her mother posed for a portrait to be painted and a model to be made from the portrait, but dates don't coincide with the age of the child and the year the doll was made.

But we see no reason why the child could not have posed for other portrait faces used by Jumeau. Carrier-Belleuse was the art director in the Jumeau factory, and we assume he worked on many of the beautiful heads. One writer suggested many Jumeau heads were merely variations of the original Long-Faced Jumeau.

Mme. Triana also remarked that the Long-Faced Jumeau's long, slightly pouty face had a family resemblance—the doll looked like a Carrier. In studying sculpture and sculptors, we have often found a sculpture resembles the artist, no matter what the artist does or who the model is. This could have been true with the Long-Faced Jumeau or other models that have the longer-face modeling.

Right: Our incised *Dèposè 9 Jumeau* is 20 inches tall. This doll, referred to as an *Incised Jumeau,* is considered older by doll experts than stamped Tête Jumeau. Doll was recently dressed in antique materials.

Three Jumeau bodies, left to right: In-cised Jumeau, E.J. and Tête. Not all Jumeau bodies are the same.

Back of Tête Jumeau body. Hole in back of head was for turnkey to open and close eyes.

Kiss-throwing Jumeau wears original clothes and Jumeau-marked shoes.

Reproduction costume and new mohair wig on antique Tête Jumeau.

Albert-Ernst Carrier-Belleuse was born June 12, 1814, and died on June 3, 1887. He studied one year at the *Ecole des Beaux Arts de Paris*, in 1840, and won a third-place medal in 1861 for his sculpture *Salve Regina*. In 1863, another sculpture, *La Bacchante*, put him in the spotlight of Europe. In 1867, he was awarded the Medal of Honor for a sculpture titled *Messie*. He was also decorated by the Legion of Honor.

Carrier-Belleuse sculpted busts of many famous Europeans, including Ernest Renan, Napoleon III and Jules Simon. His decorative sculptures were very popular during his time.

Our research makes us realize the Long-Faced Jumeau is the oldest Bébé, and the fact it is a sculpture by Carrier-Belleuse makes her desirable. This knowledge can raise the price of this already-expensive doll.

We also discovered these Bébés were made under the supervision of Emile Jumeau, not his father, Pierre François Jumeau. This provides us with a more-definite time schedule of when the dolls were made.

Right: 36" Tête Jumeau

Tête Jumeau in original costume.

Character Jumeau and her box full of information.

DOLLS IN ORIGINAL BOXES

Only once in a great while does a doll from the 19th Century show up in its original box. It is quite unexpected to find a doll completely unplayed with and in its original manufacturer's condition. Those dolls are great finds, not because there is deteriorating cardboard around them, but because they tell the true story.

Dolls in these boxes tell the collector how the doll was dressed, complete from underclothing to outer costume, including socks to marked shoes. And, they reveal the original wig materials and styles. To look even further, we can discover the original finish on the doll and see how the doll was strung in the very beginning.

The box, too, has information for the collector. Usually printed in French, it lists the company making the doll, the doll's size number, color, and material of its hair. Sometimes, information on the costume is included and even the original selling price may be marked on the box.

Over the many years we have been studying and collecting dolls, we have acquired a few dolls in their original boxes. Only three of these are French: a small Jumeau in her chemise, SFBJ boy 238, and the large Character Jumeau shown here.

The 24'' Character Jumeau box and doll bought at auction turned out to be filled with intriguing information. First we checked whether the number, size, and information matched the doll. We checked with the former owner and were told this 1890's doll was purchased in France in 1950. Michelle Tibbets who grew up in France, translated the information on the inside of the cover:

House (Maison) Of Jumeau

. . . Number one manufacturer of the world for making beautiful Bébés.

. . . Bébé Jumeau is the Best National Toy of France. In all the large (best) expositions in France and other countries, they have always been proclaimed successful. Their victories aside, these dolls have largely contributed to the resurgence of French manufacturing.

. . . Of extra superior fabrication, they (it) are unique in their genre and absolutely perfect. And our charming little girls have adopted them with joy and happiness. They have all the qualities indispensable for this perfection: beauty, durability, and lightness.

. . . The Bébé Jumeau is beautiful. It owes this

Left: Character Jumeau from original box. Doll incised 225

quality to the joyous modeling by the gracious master sculptor Carrier-Belleuse, and its head of fine porcelain possesses ideal painting which distinguishes it from all others (in its class).

. . . The Bébé Jumeau is durable — it owes this quality to its method of construction. All the body parts are made of wood or wood pulp with two essential differences, mortise and tenon jointure, which renders them impervious to atmospheric variation and...

. . . Le Bébé Jumeau is lightweight — since it must stand up to a difficult life, this light weight is obtained by reducing the weight of its parts and by a reduction, made with precision, before reuniting the two woods necessary to their construction.

. . . With all these qualities, the Bébé Jumeau places itself on the highest rung of the French manufacture, and is why it can claim the title "National Toy."

In their cartons, the Bébés were always placed with the feet on the end side of the boxes.

Garantite: The head of the Bébé Jumeau is recognized exclusive property of the House (*Maison Jumeau*) by judgment and is confirmed by the Court of Appeals of Paris.

Depot: The marking of its novel body was the object of a disposition of the Council of THE PRUD — HOMMES.

Brevetés: The design of its eyes is patented as is the box the Bébé is in. It is therefore protected from counterfeit.

The Bébé Jumeau is sold by the best maisons (*houses or stores*) of the first order.

NATIONAL TOY
BÉBÉ JUMEAU
Natural hair
Always the best buy.

Carrier-Belleuse, as stated in *The Encyclopedia of Dolls* by Coleman, died in 1878, so we must assume that the art director of the Jumeau factory and sculptor of the dolls was the son by the same name, not the father.

The box is made of quarter-inch wood boards of unknown variety, as none is exposed. It is nailed together and covered with two layers of thin paper —inside and out. The outside and bottom of the box is, or was, lavender with wood-printed tape on all corners and top and bottom edges. The inside is light green.

There is a cardboard flap on the top inside of the box. This blue flap was used so the doll would be labeled in the box even if it stood up in the box. The box's cover is of medium weight cardboard and has resisted time like the wood box itself; labels and advertising are all intact.

NOTE: Dressed dolls should not be kept in their cardboard boxes for long periods of time and the boxes shouldn't be kept in the same closed case with the doll. The chemicals in the paper cardboard will deteriorate fabrics such as silk, silk taffeta, and the like. Store the boxes away from the dolls.

You wonder, I wonder—why do we pay so much more for the doll and the box? Because the doll in the original box represents original perfection and education. Keep the doll and box as is and it can be sold for more when it is returned to the box for resale.

This is the first time we have found any mention of who created the wonderful Jumeau character dolls. We feel sure that Jumeau would not say in his advertising that the dolls were sculpted by someone who had died some 13 years earlier.

In numerous places we have found mention of Carrier-Belleuse working as art director for the Jumeau factory and of Carrier-Belleuse, father or son, being the sculptor of the Long Face Jumeau. We have found no mention anywhere of the sculpting of the interesting character Jumeau faces that were supposedly made in 1890 and after, until this time.

If this 225 24" character was sculpted by Carrier-Belleuse, then we can assume the rest of the character dolls in this series were his creations also.

The Jumeau character series may run from 200 to 224. Not all the numbers between these two have been found. There are some in the series that are not incised with numbers on the outside, but numbered inside with pencil. These doll heads, I believe, were made for the large mechanicals that were adult toys. (There are still some of these to be found in working order.) Then there must have been some of these dolls mounted on regular Jumeau bodies; these are few and far between. Just once in a great while does one come up for an extremely high price at auction.

I look at these dolls, of which I have six, and wonder why a doll sculptor would make a face

Right: Very rare No. 223 Jumeau character, 24".

Smiling Character Jumeau is No. 203.

Unhappy Character Jumeau. No number

frozen in such a distorted position. What mother would give her child a doll with that kind of face? Yet these character Jumeaux give a new dimension; they make a statement in a collection. I have selected the less exaggerated character faces to show here.

You may find them on the front cover (#223) and pages 69-75. Their sizes range from 22'' to 28''.

THE PREMIER JUMEAU

The very earliest of the Bébés made by Emile Jumeau are rightfully called "Premier Bébés. These are truly beautiful. If one is found with the original couturier costume, she is a dream come true—an expensive dream!

We present such a well preserved beauty here. She is on an eight-ball jointed body, with unjoint-

Above: Character Jumeaus and their old costumes.

Right: Crying or singing Character Jumeau, No. 211.

Premier Jumeau. 14''. In all original clothing. Marked 3.

A perfect E J 9, original costume.

Jullien doll, incised *Jullien,* is 13 inches tall and wears her original chemise.

ed wrists. Her blond wig and deep blue eyes are original. She is 12-½'' and incised with only a 4.

The costume, from undies, socks and marked turquoise shoes, are all hers. The aqua, cream and gold couturier costume is fine old satin, with a skirt double pleated of cream and turquoise. She is like a little iridescent bubble. I am almost afraid to look for fear she will float away.

E.J. JUMEAU

This wonderful Jumeau stands 20'' and is incised ''Depose E 9 J.'' Her body is stamped and has no loose ball-joints. She has applied ears. Her costume accents the lovely amber-brown rayed eyes and her delicate painting.

She is like this year's new maroon pansy, all deep red velvet, with a wonderful face. Or, maybe she is more like a little character from an 1880 book who wants to tell a story.

This doll was the star in a Theriault's auction. She had the prime place with spotlights only slightly exaggerating her beauty and fabulous original costume. She is Vernon's first Jumeau — and well worth waiting for!

Right: 20'' Jullien. Face appears to be the same mold as 29'' Jullien.

Small French dolls make an ideal collection for someone with limited space. Left to right: Bébé Louve, Jumeau, Bru, Steiner, Jullien and Jumeau. These dolls, all under 14 inches, are called *Milettes*.

JULLIEN

Jullien dolls, made in Paris from 1863 to 1904, are not plentiful, but occasionally one is offered for sale. These dolls are nice to have in a complete French collection, but we don't feel their faces have a *love-at-first-sight* appeal.

The Jullien body was made of hollow wood and advertised as being the most-solid, lightest body for a doll. Dolls were well-made with wood hands that had thin, separated fingers. All Jullien dolls are marked with the name *Jullien* on the neck, along with a size number. Some later ones had walking mechanisms, talking mechanisms and sleep eyes.

We hesitate to say it, but it appears only two models of the Jullien doll were produced. Jullien dolls all have a family resemblance.

F.G.—FRANÇOIS GAULTIER

In our search for definitive information on the maker of heads marked *F.G.*, we contacted Barbara Spadaccini, assistant curator of toys at the Museum of Decorative Arts in Paris. She translated a journal article on Gaultier written by Florence Poisson, who is curator of the Roybet Fould Museum in Courbevoie, France.

Poisson's research does not solve the mystery of the three different markings found on F.G. heads. But from different inventories, it appears François Gaultier made bisque doll heads and limbs, as well as all-bisque dolls. There is no

mention in any inventory of other doll-making materials for making complete dolls. The article suggests Gaultier supplied heads to doll makers in Paris, including Gesland, Jullien, Rabery and Delphieu, Thuillier and Vichy.

The dates below prove *François Gauthier* and *François Gaultier* are the same person. The doll maker originally used the name Gauthier, but research he did in 1875 indicated the "th" spelling was incorrect. He changed it to the correct "lt" spelling. There is *no* evidence of a *Ferdinand Gaultier*, the person doll collectors had believed was the maker of F.G. dolls.

1862—On his daughter's birth certificate, Gauthier is noted as maker of porcelain heads. In the *Commercial Directory of 1884,* publicity states the firm was founded in 1860. Information on his daughter's birth certificate confirms this date.

1867—Gauthier acquired a plot of land in St. Maurice. This was his only address after 1867.

1872—On December 2, Patent No. 97360 was taken out by François Gauthier for the improvement of molds for making dolls' heads.

1875—Legal documents give correct spelling of his name as François *Gaultier.* Until then, he had spelled his name *Gauthier* and was known by this spelling in business. The "th" spelling was due to an error he discovered when he had to re-establish family records after a fire at the town hall. The legal transcription proves François *Gaultier,* the porcelain maker, is the same person as the François Gauthier of the patent.

1881—In a legal inventory of the firm's stock following his wife's death, F. Gaultier was described as a specialist of making doll heads.

1884—Firm becomes Gaultier and Son.

1886 to 1892—François Gaultier served as mayor of St. Maurice.

1888—Firm becomes Gaultier Brothers.

1899—Gaultier Brothers becomes part of SFBJ company but not part of land or premises.

This research still does not solve the entire mystery, as far as doll collectors are concerned. Doll collectors call a doll by the maker of the

Left: Marked Jullien 11, 29". She wears her antique blue silk coat. Real hair is probably a replacement. With her, is a 11" Jullien marked 1.

Well decorated, large-eyed doll marked F.G. in a scroll. On stockin-
ette-covered Gesland body.

F.G. in a scroll. 31'' doll

Incised F 3/0 G. 14'' Gaultier doll on leather body similar to a Bru body with bisque hands.

Large-eyed François Gaultier doll. 27''. Incised F10G in a scroll.

Bébé Francais, registered by both Danel and Jumeau. Incised B10F. 22''

head, so dolls marked *F.G.* are referred to as Gaultier's. But what about a doll with a head marked *F.G.* and a body marked *Bébé Gesland?*

Heads marked *F.G.* are painted in a style of their own. None of the marked heads of Jullien, Thuillier or Rabery and Delphieu resemble the painting or colors used on F.G.-marked heads. Heads on all Gesland bodies seem to be marked *F.G.* and are painted in the same style, with the same palette of colors.

F.G. heads and dolls are valuable to a collector because they are made of fine bisque and are well-decorated. Many heads were pressed of extremely fine, translucent porcelain.

We have found three types of bodies on F.G.

dolls—wood bodies, wood-and-composition bodies and Gesland bodies. Bodies by Gesland are made of a padded metal armature covered with knit fabric. Knit-covered bodies and large, 31-inch wood-and-composition bodies have Gesland labels.

Some small, later *F.G.* dolls are not as well-painted, and bisque is not the same quality. One detail that alerts us to the difference is low painting of nostril color, which makes the doll appear as if it has a bloody nose.

SFBJ

The Société Française de Fabrication de Bébés and Jouets (French Society for the Manufacture

Right: Larger 29-inch doll is incised *SFBJ* and *13.* Sitting doll is a 27-inch SFBJ doll and stamped *Tête Jumeau.* Both dolls have open mouths with teeth. French dolls like these, made after 1900, are less expensive and less valuable in a collection.

SFBJ No. 237 doll was made in many forms—as boy or man by addition of moustache and costumes, as doll on far left shows. Face on doll on far right is similar to SFBJ No. 236 doll, but this doll has domed head.

of Dolls and Toys) was the merger of many great doll makers of France. The company was also known by its initials—SFBJ.

The company was formed in 1899 and produced dolls in Paris until 1925. Doll makers merged together in order to compete with German doll makers and to produce dolls at a lower cost to increase their profits.

Members of SFBJ included the doll-making firms of Bru, Jumeau, Fleischmann & Blödel, Rabery & Delphieu, Pintel and Godchaux, Jullien and Danel & Co. There may have been others. Dolls produced by the company were marked *SFBJ*, but often the neck mark of the individual doll maker was included. This is the reason we

Right: SFBJ No. 236 doll is 28 inches tall. Feet have been repaired, patched and poorly painted.

Left: SFBJ 238 in original box.

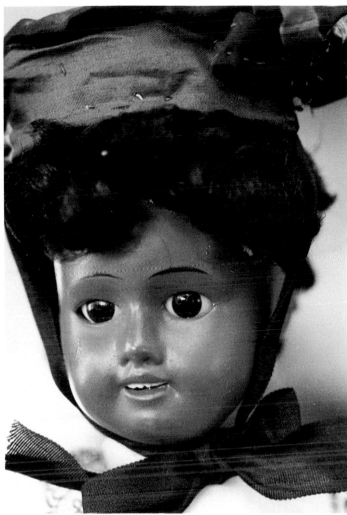

Doll is incised *Unis France*. When doll was made, work-manship and painting had deteriorated in an attempt to speed up production to compete with German doll-making companies. There are no eyelashes, and only single brow strokes were used. Doll is about 13 inches tall.

Three No. 251 SFBJ dolls. Dolls with this number were made in many sizes. Large doll is 25 inches tall; small dolls are each 9 inches tall.

find a doll referred to as an "SFBJ doll, stamped with Tête Jumeau" or other doll-maker's name. See doll on page 83.

Today, the largest number of available French dolls bear the SFBJ mark. Most SFBJ dolls had composition bodies and human-hair wigs. Some dolls were inferior and made of poor-quality bisque. The best SFBJ dolls were character dolls, which still hold charm for many collectors today.

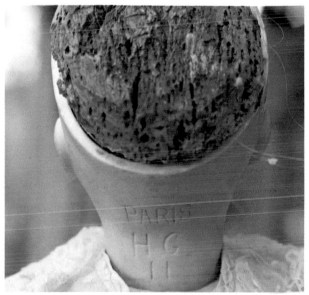

Back of doll incised *Paris HG 11*. Maker is unknown.

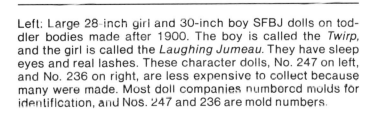

Left: Large 28-inch girl and 30-inch boy SFBJ dolls on toddler bodies made after 1900. The boy is called the *Twirp*, and the girl is called the *Laughing Jumeau*. They have sleep eyes and real lashes. These character dolls, No. 247 on left, and No. 236 on right, are less expensive to collect because many were made. Most doll companies numbered molds for identification, and Nos. 247 and 236 are mold numbers.

Later Schmitt doll is 31 inches tall and incised with crossed hammers in a shield. Bisque has more tinting than early Schmitts, and brows are wider. Costume is original.

Body of small Schmitt doll has flat behind, marked with crossed swords in a shield. Chest label is probably doll-shop label. We found doll dressed and in mint condition.

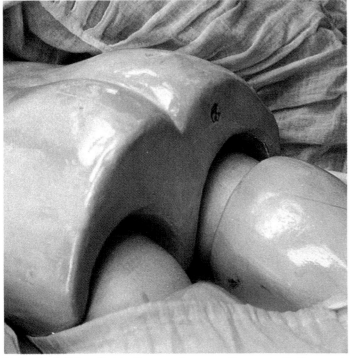

Schmitt doll has flat bottom on torso so it could sit. Crossed hammers in a shield is usually found on flat surface.

SCHMITT AND SONS

From 1863 until 1891, Schmitt and Sons made dolls in Paris. These dolls have recently become popular with collectors, and there are several reasons for this. Dolls are fine quality, and they are not plentiful. Collectors of French dolls often feel they need at least one doll made by Schmitt and Sons. The round faces of these dolls have a charm all their own.

The Schmitt body is distinctive. It can easily be distinguished from other French doll bodies by its flat bottom, which allows the doll to sit easily. The bottom is marked with crossed hammers in a shield. Other characteristics of the doll include long feet, which are usually marked with numbers on the bottom, large ball-joints in the shoulders, elbows, knees and hips, and a gauntlet-shaped forearm with no wrist joint.

Right: Early 17-inch Schmitt doll is incised with crossed hammers in a shield. She is pale bisque and has a pressed head.

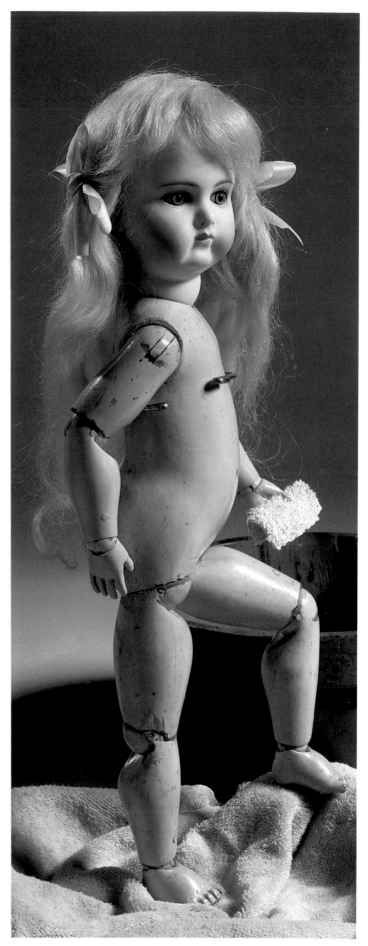

Huret doll, chins on these dolls are identification marks. They are all similar

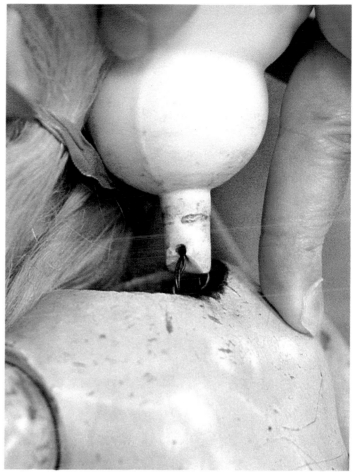

Huret is given credit for inventing the swivel-head doll. This photo shows bisque extension found on most Huret dolls. Later dolls with swivel heads do not have this porcelain extension.

These dolls did not have cork pates. Instead, heavy cardboard, often painted flesh color, was used. Dolls usually wore sheepskin wigs.

Heads had one of two markings—the incised crossed hammers in a shield or *Bte SGDG* and a size number. Dolls marked *Bte SGDG* appear to be older.

Eyebrows on Btc SGDG dolls are extremely narrow, resembling those of lady dolls. Dolls with the crossed hammers have wider brows, with softer, less-distinct hairlines. All the faces appear to have been created by the same sculptor because the dolls share a family resemblance. Some dolls were exquisitely dressed in Paris-marked costumes.

Blue and brown paperweight eyes were used, but they had less depth than other paperweight eyes. Pale-blue eyes were very attractive. The company is reported to have made one open-closed mouth doll with five teeth.

CALIXTE HURET

Huret, Maison (House of Huret) made dolls in Paris from 1850 until sometime in the 1920s. Early lady dolls by Calixte Huret were usually marked with a stamp on the chest of leather-bodied dolls. The dolls we are interested in are unmarked but easily distinguished from other dolls by their modeling.

Far left: Schmitt. Completely original. 18''

Left: Unmarked Huret doll is 17 inches tall. Head has porcelain extension from swivel neck. Doll has metal hands and all-wood body with tongue-and-groove joints that work smoothly. She also has ankle and wrist joints.

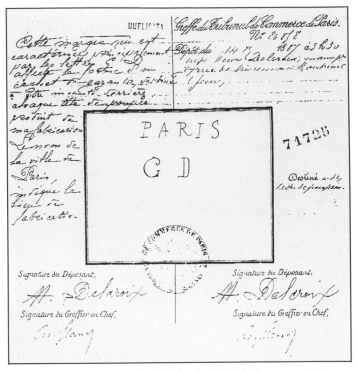

Registration of mark of Henri Delcroix. (This is important information and proof).

The faces of the Huret Bébés are distinctly modeled. They resemble the faces of Huret lady dolls made earlier. Dolls have a unique, pushed-in chin, as if they were modeled after the same face or heads made from the same original piece of sculpture. Eyes on child dolls are painted or set-in glass.

Huret originated and patented the swivel head. The first swivel heads were made like later ones, except a hollow-porcelain, tubelike extension, about 1 inch long, extended down into the body.

Heads were put on a partly hollowed-out wood body. Wood arms and legs were jointed and attached to the torso with beautifully made tongue-and-groove joints. Metal hands were added to the arms.

Not many of these dolls are available today, but they are unique and should be included in an advanced collection.

HENRI DELCROIX

Delcroix's dollmaking has not been listed along with Jumeau or Steiner, and because he didn't join the SFBJ, his name isn't as familiar. I had been collecting dolls for many, many years before the dolls of Henri Delcroix joined my "want list." That is, not until Vera Kramer moved her doll museum, Dolls in Wonderland, from England to St. Augustine, Florida.

Kramer had a doll with the mark "PAN and Paris" on it which she had purchased about 1928 in Paris. The doll was beautiful and different. You can see the doll listed and pictured under PAN in Colemans', *The Collector's Encyclopedia of Dolls, Volume 2.*

I met Vera at a UFDC convention where she told me of a pending sale of a few of the dolls in her museum. A few weeks later, I called to see if I could buy the PAN. Vera placed the doll for sale with the highest price a doll had ever been sold for at that time and stipulated that I would have to go to Florida to get the doll. We made the trip.

Whenever a high price is paid for a doll, word gets around and similar dolls seem to come out of the woodwork. To have believed that this was the only PAN, would have been folly. Once a doll is sculpted and a mold made, certainly more than one doll will be produced. It would have to be a

Incised Paris, PAN 11, 29'' doll of Henri Delcroix.

Right: PAN of PARIS. 29'' Delcroix doll

Another Delcroix doll, incised G D 1. 12"

Another little 16" PAN, incised PARIS on the top edge of the back of the head.

very unusual circumstance to cause even a *small* number of dolls to be made from the mold.

Henri Delcroix made dolls between 1865 and 1887 in Paris and other cities in France. There are many marks attributed to Delcroix: "GD Paris," " ⨂ ," "PARIS HD," "PARIS PAN." We have found dolls marked "Paris HG" and others with just the block letters "PARIS" that match what we believe to be Delcroixs.

These dolls can be identified at a glance by their large round eyes. They are of the type that once you've passed by, you do a double take. Some of the dolls have good bisque, others are acceptable. To me, the charm of the faces make up for anything else that isn't perfect.

Since our trip to Florida to pick up the PAN, we have purchased four other Delcroix dolls. We also saw one marked "PAN" at an auction that we did not buy.

We present our collection of Delcroix dolls here to add a new dimension to collecting French Bébé dolls.

Left: 27" doll incised PARIS PAN 10, in all-original costume. A favorite doll of the doll crafters.

Delcroix doll, incised only PARIS. 14"

Early Motschman-type Steiner. 18". Cobalt blue flat eyes.

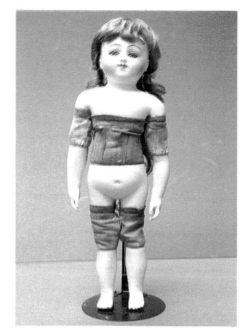

Steiner used Motschmann-type bodies on very early dolls. The porcelain body parts were joined with strips of kid and fabric.

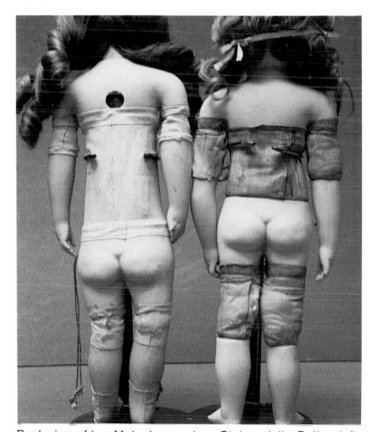

Back view of two Motschmann-type Steiner dolls. Doll on left has push squeak box in middle of body that still works. Hole in bisque is to let sound out. Doll on right has pullstring voice, which is later than squeak box.

JULES NICHOLAS STEINER

Although the name Steiner is German, Jules Nicholas Steiner was French. He produced dolls from 1870 to 1901 in Paris.

Steiner dolls may be the most fascinating to study because of the different body and head designs. You must study Steiner dolls to be able to identify them at a glance.

Dolls with variations of the Motschmann-type bodies were made by Steiner. Dolls on mechanical bodies, and the kicking or temper-tantrum-throwing doll were the most plentiful. Steiner made wire-eyed dolls with plump faces and Jumeau-type dolls on a different type of composition body.

There were several series and figures of Steiner molds. The A-series and C-series are the dolls we find most often today. These dolls are found with wire eyes and the name *Bourgoin* often stamped

Left: Brown A-series Steiner, with colored 1889 Steiner body label, has fully jointed, brown, composition body. Doll could have been made in 1889 or *any* time after.

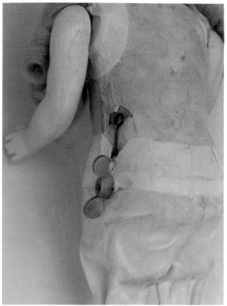

Key and turn-on lever of Kicking Steiner—mechanism is inside body. Leatherlike material of legs allows them to move.

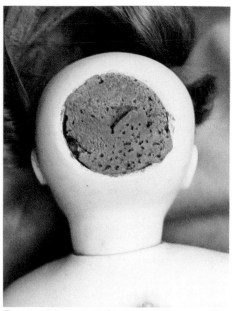

Back of head of Steiner doll is unlike usual cut-off head of French dolls. This style was probably used when manufacturers changed from shoulder-head mold to swivel-head mold.

A-series Steiner on five-piece, crude papier-mâché body. Body is not labeled but head is. From research, we know Steiner used this kind of body before using jointed, labeled bodies.

Below: 24-inch, A-series Steiner doll is stamped in red *Bourgoin* and *Steiner.*

in red behind the ear. They may also have Steiner markings on the head.

Pates on Steiners were made of pressed cardboard, not cork. Most papier-mâché bodies were made of a purple mixture. Newspapers were used to make mâché for the bodies, and old newspapers were printed with purple ink. You can see the purple color when you look in a joint where paint has worn off.

Some early heads were a solid dome. Later, Steiner used the same head with a round hole in the back to make it easier to set eyes. See the photos on page 128.

Shortly after Steiner's death in 1891, records claimed Steiner had over 30 patents for mechanized dolls, changing eye movements, talking mechanisms and combinations of movements for dolls.

We are unclear as to the exact date, but Amedee Lafosse took over the Steiner factory. Later she was followed in the Steiner Co. by a man named Lambert, who had owned the Henri Alexandre Doll Company. From 1899 to 1901, Jules Mettais was the director of the Steiner Co. Mettais also purchased the May Brothers doll

Right: Face of this Steiner doll is pleasant and nicely painted. Steiner eyes never have the depth of Bru or Jumeau eyes.

G Series Steiner. 27". Note lip modeling.

C Series Steiner. 26". Dress is beaded.

Unmarked Motschmann Steiner with cloth inserts between bisque sections. 18". Skin wig. Note thick brows and blush over eyes. Antique baby clothes, probably original.

business. In 1906, Edmond Daspres took over what originally was the Steiner Co.

The Phenix Bébé was first registered by Henri Alexandre. It was later produced by the Steiner Co. after Lambert and his successors took over.

The doll marked *Mascotte* was registered by May Brothers. It was later produced by the successors in the Steiner firm.

Dolls marked *E.D.* may also have made by the Steiner firm because Edmond Daspres was one of the successors in the Steiner Co.

After studying Steiner dolls and their variations, we feel Steiner was so creative that almost any rare thing that comes up in dolls might be attributed to him.

Study of original costumes. Schmitt, 3 Steiners, and another Schmitt.

Left: A figure Steiner even has Steiner shoes.

Phenix Bébé—Our Phenix Bébé is a large doll, about 22 inches tall. She was first produced by the Henri Alexandre Doll Company and later by the Steiner Co.

After feeling the bisque inside her head and holding it to the light, we believe the Phenix Bébé is an early doll. The pressed head is rough inside, and areas vary in thickness so translucency varies. Ears were made in a separate pressed mold, then stuck to the outside of the head while still in the greenware stage. Ears are pierced through the lobes.

Our doll came to us from the "Yesteryear Museum," located in New York. Fifteen years ago, Lillian Sproul, the owner-operator, closed the museum and sold the dolls it contained. We purchased several dolls from the museum to add to our collection.

Phenix Bébé is not often offered at auction or seen for sale. She is a rare, lovely doll, and we gladly share her with you.

Our Phenix Bébé wears her original dark-brown wig. Her curls are very long and small in diameter. Front hair is turned in three rolls toward the face, and hair is pinned in place.

Her face is blushed a little all over. Her cheeks and double chin are deeply blushed. The color appears to be pompadore, which is a china paint used to give a rosiness to cheeks.

Eyebrows are perfectly painted in medium brown. The underside of the brow is solid brown, and feathered strokes above the brow curve the same way.

Eyes are blue-gray paperweight, with fine, white lines radiating from the pupil. Black eyelashes are broken by the eyelid crease and are painted on a strong slant.

There is space between the lips, but it is painted a very soft pompadore. The upper and lower lips are blotted along the outside edge, which leaves a heavier color inside. Accent lines, as well as lips, are pompadore. Nostril color and eye dots are very small and light.

There is no black eyeliner running around the inside edge of the eyes. Instead, darker spots are used where each lash begins. This was done by drawing the pen over the edge of the eye hole as it came out to make each lash.

Left: Compare these four 12-inch bodies. From left to right: R.D. body has fat little tummy; Jumeau body has oval stamp on back; wire-eyed Steiner has body stamp on hip; Schmitt doll has unusual shaping on upper arms and upper legs.

Above: Looking into torso of large A-series Steiner shows voice box and string that operated it. Body parts were put together with leather strip.

Above: Many collectors think of C-series as the only Steiner dolls with wire eyes. This is an A series with wire eyes. Note square cutout of porcelain on rim where wood bar for eye mechanism was placed.

Above: Phenix Bébé incised with star and 94 is 22 inches tall. Her painting is delicate and light.

Marked *M3* for Mascotte, doll has abundance of lashes and very heavy brows.

Unmarked doll on linen-covered body.

Mystery doll, unmarked. On body similar to a Petit Dumontier. Has metal hands. 26". Old chemise.

UNMARKED AND UNKNOWN DOLLS

There are good-quality French dolls with no markings on head or body to indicate the maker. Advanced collectors usually like to have one or two of these in a collection. Often dolls with a solid pate and a bald head, usually called a *Belton*, fall into this category of "unmarked dolls."

Collectors also collect "unknown dolls." These dolls have initials or other markings, but their maker is unrecorded. If an unknown doll is beautiful, it is a good addition to an advanced collection.

Unmarked and unknown dolls are fine exhibit dolls. Because of their rarity, they often win ribbons. But an increase in their value is always questionable. As more research is done, it may be proved that unmarked or unknown dolls were common.

Right: Doll has no marking on head. She has a sheepskin wig, deeply blushed cheeks, mauve eye shadow and two-tone lip coloring. She is 16 inches tall.

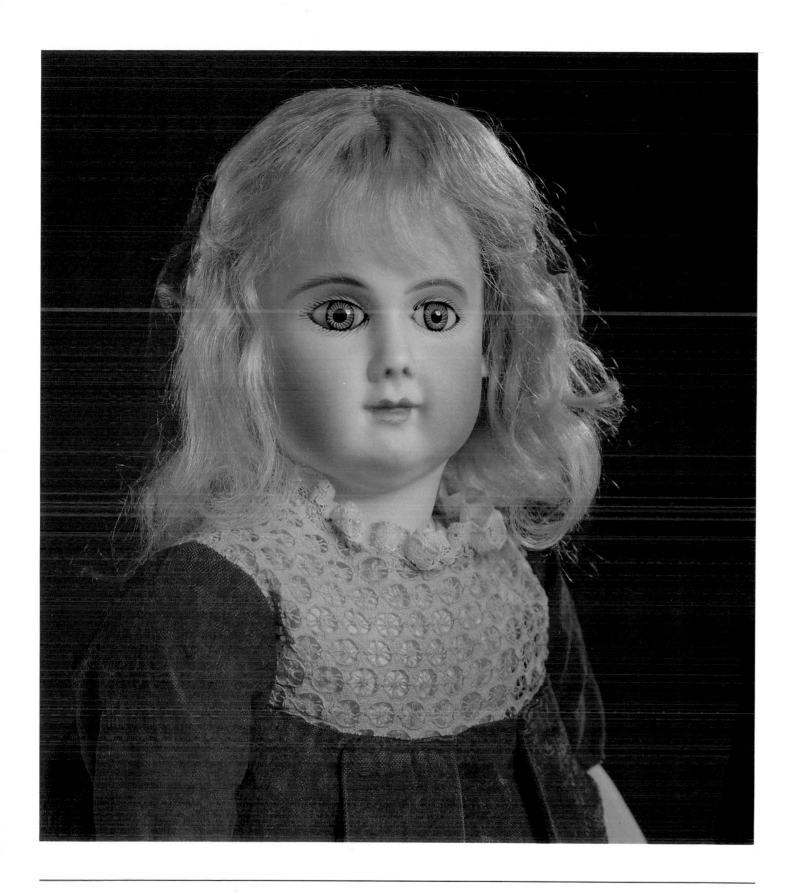

Left: These two dolls may have been made by the same maker. One has two Cs back to back, and the other is unmarked. Doll sitting in highchair is 15 inches tall. Standing doll is 16 inches tall and also shown on previous page. Both dolls have similar papier-mâché bodies. Doll in highchair is dressed as baby, and other doll is dressed as toddler. Both wear original clothes.

Above: The Mystery doll, J M. 22"

Making French Dolls — Yesterday and Today

⬧

Your enjoyment and appreciation of antique dolls will increase if you know how dolls were made and how difficulties were overcome to produce the beautiful toys we treasure today. It can also help you determine the age of a doll if you know how it was made.

Every French doll had a beginning. Like a work of art, it was usually conceived in the mind of an artist. He may have been inspired by a real child, or he may have had an idealized vision in his mind. Some dolls were not designed as children's toys to be played with. They were designed as things of beauty to appeal to adults who purchased them for children.

CREATING A DOLL

After the idea for a doll was conceived, the doll's head was modeled (sculpted) from water-softened clay in one or two sizes *larger* than the desired finished doll. Today, original doll heads are modeled in plasticine (an oil-based clay), *Sculpey* (a commercial modeling substance) or the same type of water-softened clay used by doll makers 100 years ago.

Dolls modeled by French doll artists were so perfectly sculpted that they contained no undercuts (places that would catch on the mold), and they could be made in a two piece mold.

A face section and back section of the mold were made of plaster. In our years of working with dolls and molds, we have found only two doll heads that were made in more than two pieces. These were the three-piece mold for a Heubach head, called *Baby Stewart,* and the five-piece mold of Albert Marque dolls.

Original Head—The first modeled head was the *original.* It was usually solid clay and was not fired. The original head had a plaster mold made over it, and the head was usually destroyed in the process.

When we talk about "original" dolls there is really no such thing with bisque dolls. After a mold was made from the clay model, other molds were made and thousands of heads were made from the molds.

MOLDS

Molds for French doll heads were made from plaster. We still use plaster today, but the plaster has been refined. To make a mold, the sculpture or solid-clay head is set face-up in clay in a box-like arrangement. Clay comes exactly to the halfway point on the face, so the face half of the mold can be lifted off without pulling away any detail.

A mixture of plaster and water (2-3/4 pounds

Left: Very early A4T, 15". She has leather body with lovely bisque hands. She came with trunk and extra clothing. Shoes are marked 4 A. T.

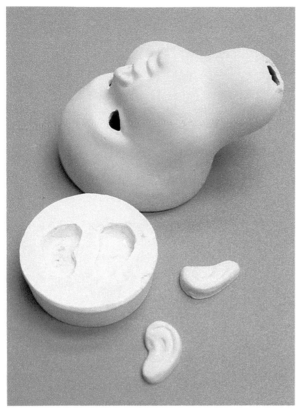

Many heads were made with applied ears. Ears were made in separate molds, then attached to head before it was fired.

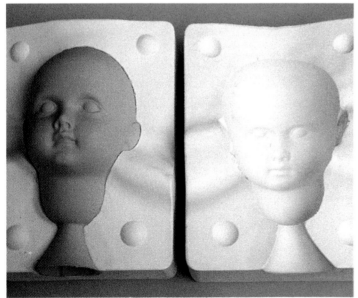

Later ears were made in mold along with head, as they are for reproduction dolls today.

of plaster to 1 quart of water) is poured over the face half of the model until the face is covered by at least 2 inches of plaster. Plaster has a chemical reaction that sets up, or becomes hard, in about 20 minutes.

Next, the box is removed, and the plaster section is turned over. The moist clay is pulled away from the mold in the back. The original clay head with plaster over the front half (face half) is set in the same boxlike arrangement. Plaster is poured over the *back* half of the head. When the plaster has set, the two mold pieces are separated.

The "original" clay head is removed and may come out in pieces or be damaged in the process. The head is usually destroyed if the mold is satisfactory. The mold is trimmed so sharp edges on the outside are smooth and plaster crumbles do not get in the slip when the mold is poured. Now we can see a doll's head, in reverse, inside the plaster shape. Next, the two pieces of the mold are strapped together.

Liquid clay (slip) is poured into the plaster mold. Plaster is used to make doll molds, and where the clay mixture touches it, the plaster quickly absorbs the water. This forms a shell in the contours of the doll head. After a 1/16-inch shell has formed inside the mold, excess slip is poured out. After an hour, the mold can be opened and the greenware (unfired porcelain) shell, in a perfect image of the original clay model, can be removed.

Master Molds—The mold process did not stop with one mold. To make thousands of dolls from one design, a *master mold* had to be made. A master mold is a mold of a mold, from which more molds are made. A master mold was made of plaster.

When we first started doll making in 1944, we used plaster or hydrocal. *Hydrocal* is a hard plaster used to make master molds in the same way as French doll makers did 100 years ago. Master molds are also called *cases*. Today, master molds are made of a liquid, rubberlike compound. When this mixture has an activator added to it, it becomes solid.

The mixture is poured over the pieces of the mold, again with mold pieces set in a boxlike arrangement. When plaster pieces are removed

Right: Small, brown-eyed Bru Breveté wears motheaten wool-challis dress. Behind her are trunk and extra clothing.

from the stiffened rubber form, half the doll head (the positive) looks up at you.

This master rubber mold, or case, is the mold used to make plaster molds for production. The rubber form is filled with liquid plaster many times. Each time, the two plaster mold pieces are pulled out and fitted together. All the molds are trimmed and dried.

Hundreds of molds can be made from one master mold before it deteriorates. This process is simpler than the old French way of making the master mold of plaster, instead of rubber.

There are modern solutions used as agents to prevent plaster or rubber from sticking to the original mold. The mold maker 100 years ago used mold soap, which is a liquid soap. Modern doll makers still use it.

Today, as well as in the 1880s, companies produce many molds by the master-mold method. The only difference is each doll company used its own molds to produce doll heads. Mold companies today make molds to sell to doll makers, hobbyists and professionals.

Most molds that are made now are made from antique dolls. A few molds are made from original sculptures.

Modern mold makers face the problem of companies that illegally use copies of molds. Molds cost a company thousands of dollars to make, and they are usually copyrighted. Copying a mold is illegal, and those who steal them are now being prosecuted. This same practice took place at the height of doll making in France and Germany. We find the same antique doll heads from different companies, and there are records of lawsuits.

The Porcelain—Making molds was only part of the procedure. Next, the doll maker had to use porcelain that would take the shape of the head, fire smooth and white, and be translucent.

Porcelain formulas were developed in Germany, and their use eventually spread across Europe. Books written at the time mention kaolin (clay) as though nothing else was mixed in. Doll makers used the term *paste* for clay and water mixed to a modeling consistency. The mixture was pressed into molds.

Ordinary clay from the ground will not make porcelain. Each doll-making firm experimented to produce fine, translucent porcelain from which to pour or press doll heads. They used a mixture of kaolin (clay), felspar (combination of minerals), quartz (mineral) and flint (siliceous rock).

Clay works better when seasoned. To season it, clay was soaked in large vats or tubs of water for as long as a year. It was then strained many times, each time through finer sieves, to remove foreign matter such as sticks, stones and lumps.

Today, porcelain formulas are still not easy to make. Clay must be gathered from all over the world. Porcelain is now made of synite (from Canada), China clay (from England), white clay (from Tennessee) and silica (from Pennsylvania). To this combination of materials, we add oxides for color and chemicals to keep the clays in suspension. *Suspension* means particles are in a solution that keeps them from settling.

Clay dug from the ground varies as the mining moves from place to place. Clays taken from near the surface contain lignite, which is supposed to burn out in firing. But we believe the lignite leaves brown specks on finished porcelain. Brown specks are also caused by metallic oxides that are so fine they go through every sieve. When fired, the oxides melt and make a brown speck on the fired porcelain.

Doll makers have always been troubled with brown specks. According to Jumeau and Bru records, it was not unusual for a company to lose 1/3 of a firing of doll heads. Today, doll makers expect 100% of the firing to be perfect.

Old doll heads were poured in white porcelain, then covered with color, but today we use a tinted mixture. Today, a doll maker buys porcelain in a gallon can, and it can be poured from the can directly into molds. We seldom think about the convenience of having slip prepared for us.

A modern doll maker complains if she has a speck on a doll, but many old dolls have specks. We know old doll-making companies culled out the worst ones. There would be few people making dolls today if they had to prepare their own porcelain slip the way French doll makers did 100 years ago.

Another convenience of modern porcelain is that it contains an oxide to precolor the bisque.

Left: This 28-inch doll has applied ears and large paperweight eyes. She has composition body with one-piece lower arms.

This saves the artist a step. It also gives us another way to determine if a doll is old or new. By looking inside the head, you can see if porcelain is white or colored. Colored porcelain almost always indicates a reproduction doll. There are very few exceptions to this rule.

We began adding color (oxides) to our porcelain because doll makers did not get an even base color over the face. Applying all-over color to the head was too difficult for most doll makers. We solved the problem by adding color to the porcelain. When other modern companies started making porcelain, they also added color. Commercial porcelains vary in color.

PRESSED HEADS

Early French doll heads were made by pressing rolled-out squares of thin porcelain paste into each half of the mold. Doll makers used this method before they discovered liquid porcelain. The two pieces of the mold, with clay in place inside, were put together and banded tightly with string.

A sponge on a stick was used to smooth clay inside the head and smooth the seam where the two pieces of the mold came together. We assume molds were open on top of the head so the worker could get inside the head to smooth the seam. Molds were closed on the top when doll makers later began using porcelain slip and molds were poured with slip at the neck hole.

POURED HEADS

To pour a porcelain doll head with slip, mold pieces were strapped together, then the mold was poured full of liquid porcelain. Slip was left in the mold for 3 to 5 minutes, depending on the size of the mold, then it was poured out. We do it the same way today.

A layer of porcelain adhered to the mold, making a shell inside it. After clay hardened for about an hour, the mold was carefully taken apart, and the fragile porcelain head was lifted out. At this point, a head was called *greenware*. French doll makers used a mold about 50 times, then discarded it. Today, a mold may last for 100 pourings.

A great deal of work still needed to be done on the head in the unfired-clay stage. Much of the quality of a finished doll head depended on what was done at this point. If the doll was to have glass eyes, eye holes were cut out. An old lithograph shows it being done 100 years ago the same as it is done today.

If an open mouth was desired, it was cut open. Teeth were also made and set in. Bumps and seam lines were cleaned at this point. Additional cleaning was done after the greenware dried. Heads were air dried, which could take 12 hours or more, depending on the weather.

The procedure is the same today as it was 100 years ago. *The Jumeau Doll Story*, by Nina Davies, published by Hobby House Press, suggests a template (a form like a stencil) was set over eyes to guide a doll maker in cutting them.

In the book, *Jumeau*, by Constance King, published by Hobby House Press, thinning clay around the eyes was mentioned. Thinning was done so glass eyes fit close in the eye hole. This procedure is important in doll making today.

When completely dry, heads are rubbed with stocking or knit material for a smooth finish. We found no mention in old books about cleaning or rubbing greenware, but we're sure it was done because most old doll heads are smooth and well-polished.

COMPARING PRESSED AND POURED HEADS

Upon close examination, you can tell if a head has been pressed of porcelain paste or poured with liquid porcelain.

Pressed Heads—If you have access to an old French doll, remove the wig and pate and feel inside the head. Can you feel ridges and uneven thicknesses made by a sponge or fingers pressing into clay? This is one sign a head was pressed.

Hold the doll up to the light. Does light come through evenly all over, or are nose and lips so thick light doesn't come through? This is another sign a head was pressed instead of poured. Most, but not all, pressed heads were made before 1890, so this helps somewhat in dating a doll.

Poured Heads—When poured with slip, a mold absorbs the water evenly on its inside surface. Clay is not thicker in the lips than elsewhere in the head. When a poured head is held to the light, light passes evenly through the entire surface.

TOP OF HEAD

The top of a French doll's head was cut off.

Right: Incised *P.4D* (Petit and Dumontier) doll is 23 inches tall. Petit and Dumontier dolls are scarce and increasing in price.

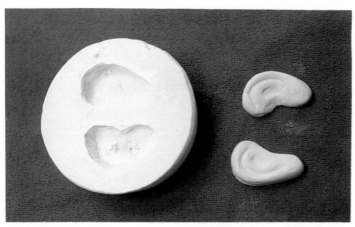

Ears on many French dolls were made in separate molds, then stuck on or applied to greenware head before firing.

that if we left a ridge on the flat part, it didn't warp. German doll makers left a heavy ridge on their porcelain dolls, probably to prevent warpage.

EARS

Many times a mold maker was uncertain of his molding ability, so he cut ears off the original model and made a separate mold of them. Ears were pressed or poured with liquid clay and applied to the moist clay head as it came from the mold. We use the term *applied ears* to describe ears attached to the head after it was formed in the mold.

You can determine if ears are applied by looking for mold lines. *Mold lines* are marks left where the two pieces of the mold come together. When ears were applied, the mold line comes straight down the side of the doll's head, and ears have the appearance of being stuck on. If in doubt, look inside the head. If the doll has applied ears, there is no indentation where the ear was in the mold.

On a head molded with ears in place, the mold line runs down the head from the center top of the ear, around the edge of the ear, off the lobe and down the side of the face. Today, reproduction dolls are made with ears in the mold, and you can usually see a mold line.

After you examine different ears and understand how they were made, you should have little trouble distinguishing applied ears from poured-in-the-mold ears.

Today, many books suggest applied ears were used only on large dolls, but this is untrue. Our 15-inch E.J. Jumeau has applied ears.

Modern reproduction dolls do not have applied ears. Even if an antique doll had applied ears, today's molds are made over the ears. We make molds and have made hundreds of them. If a doll has applied ears, we fill in around the ear with enough clay so the mold will release (come off) the antique head.

Dolls made from molds that originally had applied ears take more time for the doll maker to clean around the ear. For instance, one antique portrait doll has applied ears. We made the mold with ears so it was easier for modern doll makers to work on the head.

Some researchers believe this was done to decrease the weight of the doll for shipping. Others say it was done to protect the doll from breaking. The top of the head was the most vulnerable spot. These could be reasons, but our guess is that it was done to allow doll makers to smooth the clay when pressing the head from paste and to set eyes more easily. Only a doll maker knows how hard it is to get into a closed head or into a small hole on top of a head to set eyes.

We were the first modern doll makers to take French dolls apart and make molds of them. We believed a doll's head should be poured from the top, so we left the top of a poured head open the same way as for pressed doll heads. We studied old lithographs of later doll factories and found pictures of molds with small, centered holes so heads could be poured from the neck.

We then made molds that could be poured at the neck hole. We cut off the top of the head *after* the mold was open, while clay was still soft.

You might wonder if it makes a difference if a doll's head is poured through the neck or top of the head. It does. Porcelain clay sets up the instant it comes in contact with plaster. When pouring from the back of the head, porcelain first strikes the face. This leaves streaks on the face. When clay is poured from the neck, it strikes the top surface of the head first. This is also streaked, but the top of the head is cut out to make the head opening. French doll makers cut the head opening to the thickness of the clay all around the head.

Doll makers lost a large percentage of heads to warpage, so they sometimes used dolls with warped heads. When we made heads, we found

Right: This 16-inch F.G. doll has dark brows and dark, curly hair of unknown substance. She has well-developed, all-wood body.

FIRING

To fire greenware heads, French doll makers used huge, wood-fired kilns that took 25 to 30 hours to reach 2300F (1250C). Heads were piled on a *gazette*, which was a grill-like arrangement. The gazette was covered with a thin sheet of un-fired porcelain. While firing, the porcelain sheet shrank, along with heads, and prevented warping and cracking because heads could move with the porcelain sheet.

Even today, we have problems with shrinking and warping, so we tested something similar. We set each head on a thin, dry sheet of porcelain. The sheet shrank, along with the heads, and prevented warping. When we visited Syracuse China Co., we found they used hydrated alumina, which allowed pieces to shrink and move while firing. Hydrated alumina is similar to minute beads, which act as rollers to let pieces move as they shrink.

Porcelain is fired to 2300F (1250C), which is white hot. The inside of the kiln and each head must reach this temperature to mature, or a mottled effect may appear after the china is painted and fired again.

French doll makers were plagued with *mildewing*, a mottled effect, as are modern doll makers. When the maturation point is reached (when the temperature reaches 2300F), clay is vitrified, which means the porcelain undergoes a chemical change. After the chemical change, porcelain can never be made to return to clay and water. It is like baking a cake—the cake can't be returned to sugar, flour, eggs and milk.

Porcelain heads are like fine china dishes but without glaze. After firing, porcelain is called *bisque* or *porcelain bisque*. When we speak of collecting bisque dolls, we mean unglazed-porcelain dolls.

Doll makers today have a simplified firing process, compared to the old wood-stoked furnaces French doll makers used. We had only been making dolls a short time when we discovered a ceramic kiln is unsuitable for firing doll heads, even though it fired to 2300F (1250C). Tiny particles of glaze and clay, left from the ceramics, circulated in the kiln and adhered to the porcelain during the firing process.

Large ceramic kilns were not appropriate for doll making either. Usually we fire only a few heads at a time, so we had a smaller doll kiln made with controls for turning itself off at the *exact* moment of maturity of the porcelain. This was done by using a small pyramid of clay, called a *cone*, that melts and breaks the circuit.

After heads are cooled, they are polished by rubbing with the finest sandpaper or a scrubbie to remove outside roughness or grit. A *scrubbie* is a foam pad with a rough side, like sandpaper. Fine sandpaper was used by the French doll makers a hundred years ago.

PAINTING

China paints, or oxides, used to decorate dolls must be able to withstand 1300F (700C). Paint must melt and become part of the porcelain. We use the same oxides today as French doll makers used 100 years ago, except today's paints are ground and purified even more. Most colors we use come from one company, Reusche & Co. of Newark, New Jersey. Other companies buy from them, mix their own colors and add their label.

Some china paints are premixed with oil. We made premixed ones by grinding oxides and adding mineral oils, but they still needed more mixing with a palette knife before applying to bisque.

After firing and polishing, antique doll heads were painted with two or more coats of flesh color. This was painted on or poured over the heads. You might find a thumb mark of the painter near the neck hole where the head was held or near the rim of the head where the painter held the head.

The coating of flesh-colored paint had to be heated (lightly fired) to set the paint before the rest of the face could be painted. This step is eliminated in modern doll making by using pre-tinted porcelain, which has eliminated uneven coloring. Coating was a problem for doll makers.

Dry china paints were mixed with oil on a glazed palette. Today we often use a glazed tile. A small, flat knife, such as a palette knife, was used to mix and grind colors into the oil to make a consistency similar to toothpaste.

When we mix colors, the palette knife is used flat, in a circular motion against the tile, to grind color granules into the oil. Even the tiniest bit of unground color will leave a speck on the doll. We discovered this through trial and error. We believe this is how tiny flecks of color appeared on antique heads.

Left: Incised SFBJ dolls. Boy doll, No. 235, is on left, and girl doll, No. 238, is on right. Both are 17 inches tall.

Seeley reproduction doll shows fine lines achieved using croquill pen and china paint mixed with pen media.

On antique and reproduction dolls, cheek blush is usually the first part of the face to be decorated. Blush was applied with a light, gentle up-and-down dabbing motion, called *pouncing*. A *pounce*, which is a hard wad of wool inside a china-silk cover, was used. Pounces have been used for over 100 years.

We developed an easier way to achieve the same delicate blend of colors. We oil the face, then use two brushes—a large one and a small one—to apply color on cheeks. Color is applied with a small brush, then the large brush is used to spread it.

Pompadore is the color used on cheeks and lips. It is thinned with painting medium and applied to cheeks with the small brush. The big brush is used to spread the color with an up-and-down motion. A very fine facial sponge can also be used to apply cheek color.

There are many reasons you should know about the colors used on dolls and how old dolls were decorated. Very old dolls, made around or before 1885, had a mauve blush added above the eyes from the lid to the brow. Following the mauve-shading era, there was a time when a shading of cheek color was used above eyes. This was followed by a period when no shadow was used over eyes. You can't date dolls exactly by the color of their eye shadow, but it does give a time range.

Eye shadow is applied at the same time cheek blush is applied. Most people fire a doll's head after the cheek blush is applied, before brows and lashes are added.

Brows, lashes and lips were painted next, which took a great deal of skill. The Jumeau Co. prided itself in having girls trained to do this perfectly. Today, artists are as good or better. We found there is no easy way to do eyebrows—you must practice making strokes until they are perfect.

It's interesting to study the painting of eyelashes of old dolls. Often you find one eye has lashes that are pointed on top. The other eye has lashes that are blunt on top. This occurred because the painter did not bother to turn the doll upside down. The right eye was easier to paint from the inside out and the left from the outside in.

In an attempt to paint lashes, we found an extra-fine croquill pen was the solution for many doll artists. In reading about doll making, we found a mention of a quill being used by doll makers—a croquill pen seemed like the next best thing to us! We found fine accent lines for lips can also be put on with this pen.

We discovered another trick doll makers used that took us time to perfect. An antique doll's lips have a soft, delicate blend of color that is hard to duplicate. We found that after applying lip color, we could achieve the same softness if we blotted part of the color off with tissue.

All the best dolls had dots of color in tear ducts and nostrils. With some very old dolls, artists used two shades of pompadore for painting nostrils.

When painting was complete, the doll head

Right: *Chipmunk-faced* P.D. doll is 19 inches tall. P.D. dolls are difficult to find, but their different face design is welcome in a collection. Dress and bonnet are old but probably later than doll. Note metal hands.

was fired again. After the final firing, the head was sanded very lightly. Today we use a worn-out scrubbie for this step.

Doll Paint—In selecting French dolls, you need to know something about the paint used in the decorating process. Colors on a doll's face became permanent when they were fired. Paint can never be washed off. It can only be worn off by rough play or scraping.

If color washes off the face of a bisque doll, the face has been repaired or repainted. When repairing a bisque doll, do *not* refire the head. Any painting done after the doll is fired is surface color—there are *no* exceptions to this.

Heads of antique dolls were made of white porcelain. Modern reproduction dolls are made from porcelain that is tinted with a flesh color. The color varies, depending on which company's porcelain is used. To get an all-over color, antique heads were dipped in color or color was poured over them from two to five times. This gave a very delicate tint to the "skin." Pouring color over the head made all-over color of the dolls vary from very pale to quite ruddy.

Lip color was painted with a brush called a *cat's tongue.* It was a flat brush that held enough paint to do the lips of a large doll without having to refill it. Doll makers used sable cat's-tongue brushes in several sizes.

The artistic style of lashes and brows of French dolls make them superior to German dolls. It took skill and practice to achieve the beauty of the fine painting found on French dolls.

Lashes and brow lines were painted with a quill or very fine brush. In today's reproduction French dolls, eyebrow and eyelash painting make the doll good or bad—the work of a skilled artist or an amateur. Today, lines are made with a croquill pen or fine brush.

Two types of paint were used to paint antique French dolls. *Mat paints* were flat or dull. *Gloss* or *luster paints* were shiny. As a rule, dolls made before 1890 were entirely painted with mat colors, and dolls made after 1890 could have had some gloss paint used. German doll makers used gloss in their mixture for eyebrows in the 1890s, and some French doll-making companies used a little gloss on the lips.

Accent lines on the lips—the fine, darker-red lines at the top and bottom of the lip color—were added with a quill or very fine brush.

Colors used on bisque heads have changed over the years. Early heads were pale flesh tones because fewer washes were used. More color was used on dolls made after 1890, and the tone of the bisque became richer and darker. Lip and cheek colors were paler and softer on earlier dolls. Doll makers may have been copying the pale, unhealthy French children.

Later dolls had rosier cheeks and lips were a little darker. After 1910, there was a period of bright colors. Cheeks were rosier, and lips were bright. Color changed from fine, soft pompadore to an orange cheek blush and glossy, orange-red lips.

In the earlier years of the master doll makers, such as Bru and Jumeau, lips were painted and color was blotted to give a soft effect. After 1910, lips were painted a solid color by some doll makers. Details like these can help you decide the age of a doll just by looking at her.

China colors used in doll painting have their own names. To speak the language when discussing painting bisque dolls, you need to know the basic colors. Pompadore is the color used on cheeks and lips. Common brow colors are finishing brown, yellow-brown and gold. Dark flesh, light flesh and Oriental flesh were used for skin tones. Sometimes gloss and mat colors were mixed to give a hint of shine.

Painting is done the same way today as it was in the past. Colors are natural oxides mixed with flux. Flux is soft glass that melts at about 1300F (700C), which is the firing temperature for china painting. During firing, oxides mixed with flux become part of the porcelain.

Blush color, used above eyelids, can also be an indication of the age of a doll. A very old French doll, made before or around 1885, often has mauve blushing over eyes. This color is almost impossible to duplicate on a reproduction doll.

None of the trends in painting came or went at any exact time. For instance, you can find Long-Faced Jumeaus with mauve blushed lids and also with light-pompadore lids. The doll is also found with no lid blushing at all. This indicates the long period during which the Long-Faced Jumeau was made.

Different painting trends, problems in mold making and the art of making porcelain are things you must be able to recognize if you wish to be an expert on French dolls. All these things

Left: Long-Faced Jumeau is 29 inches tall. She was dressed about 40 years ago

affected the dolls, and knowing about them will affect your appreciation of a doll.

GLASS EYES

Glass eyes for antique dolls were made separately, then mounted in the head. A hundred years ago, eyes were made by the doll company

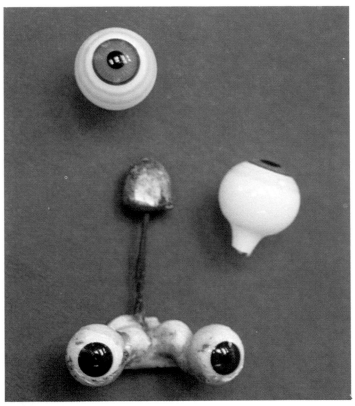

Most German dolls have round, blown-glass eyes that are hollow inside. Blown-glass eyes are used with rockers to make weighted sleep eyes. When French doll makers began using sleep eyes, they used rounded eyes instead of paperweight eyes.

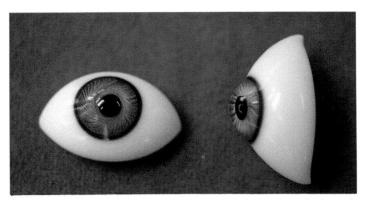

All French paperweight eyes are oval, with a deep bulge of crystal over pupil and iris to give depth.

or imported from another country, usually England. With reproduction dolls, good eyes are a problem.

It's essential to be able to differentiate between eyes used in antique dolls. You should also know how eyes were made. You need to be able to recognize different eye shapes and understand the reasons they are different.

There were three main types of glass eyes made for antique dolls. Round glass eyes, oval eyes and paperweight eyes were used for dolls. A detailed discussion of each follows.

Round Glass Eyes—Eyes are round and hollow, like tiny Christmas balls. Each has a little tube-like projection from the back, where the blowing tube was broken off. These eyes came in many colors and sizes and were usually produced in Germany for use in German dolls with sleep eyes. Round eyes were also used in very late (after 1900) French dolls when doll makers began using sleep eyes. Today, these eyes are again being made in West Germany by Reinhold Lesch. Old eyes are sold by Schoepfer in New York City.

Oval Eyes—Antique oval eyes are opaque white and shaped like a fat almond. The iris and pupil were added to the white glass while it was still molten. These eyes were often cobalt blue—they are not interesting eyes. Some very old eyes were jet black and called *pupil-less.* Actually they were irisless.

Paperweight Eyes—Paperweight eyes are the deep, beautiful eyes used in most French dolls. They are also basically almond-shaped, with a bulging lens of crystal-clear glass over the pupil and iris. Some eyes have fine, white, radiating lines in the iris, and others have a feathering in the iris. Most eyes are lighter around the pupil and have a darkened ring on the outside of the iris. These eyes have great depth.

Paperweight eyes were developed by a manufacturer in Bristol, England, in 1860. The Steiner and Jumeau companies later made their own eyes. Steiner eyes never were as beautiful as those by Jumeau. Bru eyes are different from Steiner and Jumeau, so we assume Bru made their own eyes.

Dolls with paperweight eyes can be easily distinguished from dolls with other eyes by looking

Right: Freckles is 17 inches tall and incised *Bru Jne 5.* We gave her her name because of iron-oxide specks on her nose. She has blue paperweight eyes, and her auburn mohair wig is probably original. Dress is a replacement.

at the doll from the side. See photo on page 170. With paperweight eyes, crystal bulges over the eye and is obvious, especially in larger dolls.

Gus Schoepfer, 99-years-old and still living in New York City, is the only doll glass-eye-maker in the United States. We also know a couple of men whose wives are doll makers who are experimenting with the old processes for making glass eyes.

Making Paperweight Eyes—From our discussion with Gus Schoepfer, and an early translation of a Jumeau factory tour by J. Cusset, we have a general idea of how paperweight eyes were made.

Gas jets were used to melt the glass. On the end of a glass tube, a little circle of black glass was melted and turned to make a pupil. To make the iris, a circle of blue, brown or the desired color of molten glass was circled around the black. This was done in the heat of the flame and was turned constantly to keep it round.

Threading or feathering was put in the iris of the eye at this point with tiny threads of white glass. Whether irises were left alone or had swirled lines in them made the difference in whether eyes would have rays or feathering.

Next, white opaque glass was melted and placed in a mold to make eyes the same size and shape. The molten, white, opaque glass was pushed aside with a special tool, and the pupil and iris were set in. The eye was heated again, and a drop of clear liquid glass was dropped over the iris and pupil. This gave the eye depth.

We became more intrigued with the process of paperweight eye making every time we talked with Gus Schoepfer. Schoepfer started his eye-making business in an $8-a-month rental store in 1907. We asked him to tell us how he became an eyemaker. He wrote us the following letter:

I started working in 1907 at 13 and learned how to make bird and animal eyes. I earned $3 a week for 10 hours a day, working for the Bess Co. under Gus Roehr. Then my sister and I started working piece work. We made $10 to $12 a week. In 1907, the Bess Co. went out of business. I looked for another job, but there were no other eyemakers in this country. I had saved $75.

My father made me a crude Bunsen burner, and I started in business in my mother's living room. Our apartment was small—a kitchen, three bedrooms and a parlor.

After being in business for 5 years, I traveled to Germany in 1912 to learn how to make artifical glass eyes for people. When I returned, I brought some glass dolls' eyes with me and tried to show them to doll makers. Doll makers made cheap dolls with painted eyes, so I wasn't successful with doll's eyes until 1919 and 1920.

At that time, I went to Fulper Pottery in Flemington, New Jersey. As far as I know, Fulper was the first person to make a bisque doll head in this country. My first order from Fulper was for $20,000 worth of round and oval eyes.

Then other companies began using glass eyes. Among these were Horsman, Ideal Toys and Century Dolls. Well, I bought up all the round and oval eyes from Germany I could, but Fulper went out of business. I still have a lot of eyes I bought between 1919 and 1921. I believe I have over a million pair.

Mr. Schoepfer didn't tell us he was an inventor, but we discovered he designed a mechanism for sleep eyes and had it patented. He was also a former director of the American Olean Tile Co.

Wire-Eyed Dolls—Along with different eye colors, doll-making companies experimented with eye mechanisms to open, close and move eyes. Many mechanisms were unsuccessful.

One of the most interesting mechanisms was the *wire-eyed doll*, developed by Jules Steiner. It opened and closed eyes by use of a lever behind the ear. Jumeau, Bru and other companies also had variations for closing eyes or moving them from side to side. Jumeau used a key and a hole in the back of the head.

New developments required an eye that was shaped differently. The paperweight eye, with its bulge of crystal, couldn't be used because eyes would not move. Steiner made a round, ceramic eye with an indentation for setting in the iris and pupil. These eyes didn't have a front bulge, and they opened and closed only with a

Left: This A11T has mismatched brows. Her mouth has a light line between lips. Wig style is similar to old Bru wigs.

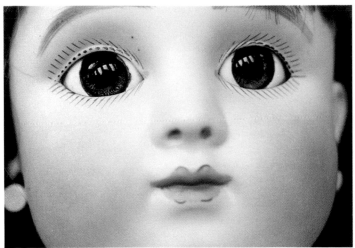

Wire eyes of Steiner doll. Eyes are made of porcelain, with glass inset for iris and pupil.

Lids are painted. Eyes close when lever behind ear is pushed down.

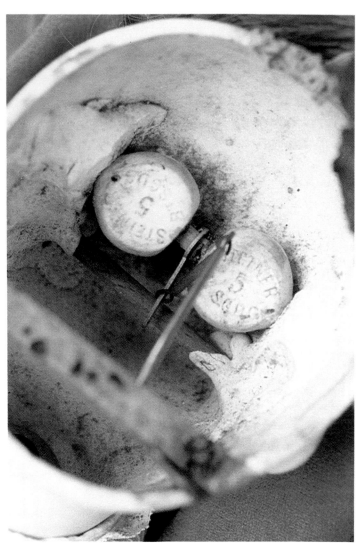

Porcelain eyeballs were marked with name *Steiner* and size. Sometimes Steiner dolls had no other markings.

lever. Steiner incised his mark on the *back* of these eyes. See photo above right.

The sleep eyes of some dolls have been replaced with set eyes. A Steiner doll that has two square cuts out of the top edge of the head rim once had wire eyes. Most wire eyes were used on C-series Steiner heads. They were marked in red with the name *Bourgoin*. We have also found two Steiner heads from the A-series with wire eyes.

A Jumeau head with movable eyes often had a round hole in the bisque in the center back. Or an inverted T-shaped hole was used in which a knob was moved to open and close eyes.

Reproduction Eyes—For many years, when we taught reproduction doll making, there was no way to reproduce eyes. We encouraged our stu-

dents to paint eyes in the bisque, then glaze them, but this was a poor substitute for beautiful glass eyes.

European eye makers now make blown glass eyes and plastic eyes, and these eyes could be used by doll makers for reproduction dolls. But we still didn't have eyes similar to the antique paperweight ones to use in French dolls.

French dolls without paperweight eyes lose a great deal of charm, so we continued to experiment. We made a mold of round eyes, then glazed and painted them. It was hard work, but a good doll artist could make exceptionally fine eyes. But it still wasn't satisfactory because eyes did not look authentic.

We kept looking for something we could substitute for paperweight eyes. One day, we used

Right: Closeup of P.D. doll shows how close together her eyes are. They seem closer together than eyes of other dolls.

epoxy on an outside table. When we moved the table, my hands felt little bumps under the edge. I looked under the table and saw the epoxy had dripped and hardened like the crystal on paperweight eyes. That gave me an idea.

We took our homemade ceramic eyes and the round, German glass eyes and added a drop or two of epoxy over the iris and pupil. It took some experimenting, but we finally discovered that if we turned the eyes down, then up again a few times, the epoxy would harden with the right bulge.

For many years these eyes worked because there were no others. Now, beautiful glass paperweight eyes are made in England. Their new eyes rival the old in beauty. There are also plastic eyes made. Don't ever consider plastic eyes for French dolls.

Setting Eyes—Setting eyes today is done exactly the same way as it was done in old dolls. A little wax is put around the inside of the eye hole to hold the eye in place and keep plaster from running through to the face. Wax acts as a seal.

After eyes have been put in eye holes lined with wax, they are adjusted so they look at you. Then plaster is spooned over the *back* of the eyes. There is a reason for setting eyes this way. If they get broken or are incorrectly set, they can easily be removed.

Do not buy a French doll as an investment without looking inside the head. If eyes have been changed, you can usually tell by the plaster marks inside the head.

You may also be able to determine if eyes have been changed by studying their shape. If eyes are round, blown German eyes, a little tube protrudes from the plaster inside the head. If they are almond-shaped, very little plaster will cover them. A good French doll should *only* have almond-shaped paperweight eyes.

One exception to using paperweight eyes was Steiner, who made a different type of eye. Mechanisms in Steiner heads were marked with his name. Dolls with these eyes are called *wire-eyed Steiners*.

DOLL BODIES

Jointed composition bodies were first produced in the late 1870s by French and German doll makers. Many collectors believe leather bodies are older than composition or papier-mâché bodies, but this is not always true.

Many companies made leather and composition bodies. The Bru Co. made composition bodies and used them for their dolls, but most Bru dolls had leather bodies. Jumeau first made lady dolls on leather bodies, then changed to papier-mâché. Steiner first made Motschmann-type bodies, then changed to composition and papier-mâché. Motschmann bodies have an upper chest, lower arms, legs and hip sections of porcelain joined by cloth or leather.

Doll collectors often use the term *composition* for jointed bodies when they should use the term *papier-mâché*. In most books, these terms are interchangeable. The only major difference between composition and papier-mâché is the addition of wood particles to papier-mâché to make composition. (Wood particles strengthen the material.)

From translations of an article describing a trip through the Jumeau factory, we discovered Jumeau used cast-iron molds to make body parts. Workers put paste-covered paper, layer by layer, into metal molds. Paper was tamped solid with a special wood tool, then half-body pieces were taken out and the halves glued together.

Wood bars were added across the chest to give larger dolls strength. Wood bars acted as an anchor to hold elastic from the legs and to fasten wire from the head. Smaller wood bars were glued inside, across the lower arm and lower leg. These bars were used to hold the metal hooks that protruded through the wood cuvets. (*Cuvets* are cuplike shapes that reinforce the top of each joint to make it work smoothly.) Wet bodies were set to dry in *hundles*, which were wicker cages.

Next, body pieces were painted white or deep pink, then several coats of flesh-colored paint were added. Finished bodies were varnished. You must *never* wash a papier-mâché or composition doll body—the finish will wash off.

Most bodies are gray underneath paint, but Steiner bodies are purple. We finally concluded that Steiner used printed newspaper for bodies, and the purple came from purple ink in the mixture.

Left: Wired-eyed 15'', Steiner Bébé incised sie C O. Unusual to find French doll dressed as baby. Doll and costume are in unplayed-with condition.

Wood cuvets (concave wood disks) were inserted in leg and arm joints of composition bodies to hold ball-joints in correct position. These are not found on reproduction bodies.

Most jointed doll bodies were assembled or strung with round fabric-covered elastic of appropriate size for the body. A few dolls, such as the Paris Bébé, were strung with springs instead of elastic.

Reproduction Bodies—When we began making reproduction dolls, we put them on cloth or leather bodies because we had no way to make composition bodies.

We made molds of bodies, then poured them in porcelain. But porcelain bodies were heavy, and pieces knocked against each other and broke. And the bodies were not authentic because French doll makers didn't use porcelain bodies.

After a great deal of searching, we located casting materials used to make store mannequins. We contacted rubber companies in an attempt to find materials that would have some "give" to improve the mannequin material.

Finally, through experimentation, we developed a compositionlike material that could be poured into a plaster body mold. This process was similar to pouring porcelain, except bodies had to be dried, not fired. We called the mixture *Milvex*. It's a very hard substance and must be sanded after drying. It can be painted with a rubber-based paint. Several companies now advertise a similar mixture for making composition bodies for reproduction dolls.

You can distinguish reproduction bodies from antique bodies just by the surface, even though they are made from the same molds. Bodies made of Milvex or similar materials can be washed.

Joints can also be used to determine if a body is old. New bodies are hard, and no cuvets are needed in arm or leg joints. New bodies are usually strung by inserting a washer on the end of the elastic, which does not pull through the leg hole. The washer is pushed in sideways and flips over when you pull the elastic. No bars are added in new bodies. Otherwise, new bodies are strung in the same way as old ones.

If a voice box is added to a reproduction doll, it is added through a trap door in the back of the composition body. This is usually done *before* composition is completely hard, when the material is only partially dry.

Many antique heads are fastened to the body by a spring in the head. A hook goes down through the neck and hooks onto body elastic or the chest crossbar. In a lithograph of a doll factory, found in King's *Jumeau* book, a machine is shown that we believe helped the worker compress the spring to get the pin through the top loop of the spring.

Doll companies made thousands of dolls and modern doll makers make only a few, but the same spring arrangement is still available. You can usually distinguish the old spring arrangement from a new one by the darkened color of the wood washers. Other washers used in old dolls were very thin and possibly made of tin. The one we use today is thick and made of iron.

PUTTING WIGS ON DOLLS

The pate and wig finish the doll body and head. A shaped pate, which covers and rounds the section on the top of the head, is made of cork. Steiner and Schmitt dolls are exceptions. Steiner used purple cardboard, similar to the mixture he used in bodies. Schmitt used heavy papier-mâché, and the pate on Schmitt dolls was usually painted a flesh tone, like bodies. There are a few other exceptions, such as the Belton-type doll that has a solid-bisque, dome-shaped head.

Right: Closeup of SFBJ dolls shows similarities between boy doll and girl doll. Mouths are similar, but boy doll has closed head with flocked hair. Both have "jewel" eyes, which are sparkling paperweight eyes. Bisque is unusually fine for SFBJ dolls.

Wigs were made of human hair, angora goat hair or mohair. Old French wigs were beautifully designed and came in many styles. The wig was usually nailed to the cork pate. On Belton-type dolls, the wig may have been tied through head holes with string or ribbon.

When we buy French dolls, we usually find the wig and pate are loose. This is to allow the buyer to inspect the inside of the head. Doll dealers never glue a wig back down, but tape may be used to anchor a pate. Hair is fastened to the pate.

Dolls look better with the wig glued down, so when a doll is yours and you're sure a wig is best for her, the wig can be lightly glued in a couple of places. Use white glue so the wig can be removed if necessary.

Reproduction pates may be carved cork but are often made of Styrofoam. It is difficult to tell new cork from old cork.

New hairstyles of human-hair wigs are similar to old wigs. We have used beautiful human-hair wigs for reproduction dolls or as replacement wigs for old dolls. Now, we can obtain real mohair from the Angora goat. This makes wonderful soft wigs that look much the same as the antique wigs.

When we first started making reproduction dolls, wigs were almost impossible to find. We experimented with human hair, mohair and even used hair from a long-haired goat.

Today, doll makers don't have this problem. Doll wigs are made in the United States, France and Korea. New wigs are made on a netlike cap, which is similar to the construction of old wigs. Soft, silky old mohair is easy to distinguish from new synthetic hair, but with human hair wigs it is almost impossible to tell the difference between them.

DRESSING A DOLL

Old dolls were dressed in a *chemise*, which is a plain commercial dress, or sent to a dressmaking department for an elaborate costume. For more information on dressing dolls, see *Doll Costuming*, published by Scott Publications. Today, dolls are dressed by their makers or costumed by women who specialize in this art.

Incised Eden Bébé Paris N. 24"

DOLL-MAKING

Now that you have followed the procedure used in making an old doll all the way from the original modeled head to the finished production doll, you will know what to look for in selecting antique French dolls. You will be able to tell what is old, new or changed on the old doll. You'll be able to determine if a doll is a reproduction doll or reproduction parts are used on an old doll. You may need to reread some parts if you have never made a doll.

We would like to recommend that you make at least one bisque doll on a composition body, preferably a French doll. There are doll studios in most major cities. After reading books on doll making, many people have made dolls without further help or advice. The process of making a doll will enlighten you about the time and effort that goes into creating one of these beautiful treasures. You will appreciate the fine painting and understand how porcelain bisque was made. You may also better understand and accept the flaws an old doll may have.

Left: Marked SFBJ 233 Paris is a 23" variation from old Jumeau character mold 211.

Parts of French Dolls

Most collectors like to think of a doll as a total entity, with a beautiful face, well-arranged hair and a perfect body covered by beautiful antique clothing.

As a buyer or collector of expensive French Bébés, you must be able to recognize and distinguish between different marks of French doll-making companies. This will help you determine if a doll is correctly identified.

You must also know what is under the wig and costume. You must be able to determine if body parts belong together. By studying parts, you will be able to determine when a doll was made—at the beginning of the period of the French Bébé, in the middle or at the end.

As a collector, you will find it easier to identify dolls if you have studied their parts and are able to identify and recognize differences. Study the photographs we include in this section, and compare the parts shown with your dolls or ones you intend to purchase.

Knowledge of dolls will make doll collecting a more exciting hobby.

DOLL HANDS

Usually a Bébé with a composition body has composition hands. Composition is a combination of ground wood, paper pulp, glue and other materials that doll companies did not disclose. When hands are painted, it's difficult to distinguish between papier-mâché (made of paper and glue) and composition. But papier-mâché hands are easily broken.

We often classify papier-mâché and composition together because we cannot distinguish between the two in a photo. French doll-making companies used composition or papier-mâché for some portion of their doll-body production.

The early Bébé had no joint in the wrist. The forearm went to the elbow joint. Hands on all French dolls were larger than those of German dolls. French doll hands were in better proportion for a child doll.

Sometimes dolls' hands seem too large to be graceful. Larger dolls had hands with separated fingers. Some very small French dolls had fingers modeled together.

Left: Doll on left is 19'' tall and incised Bru Jne 8. Two Bru Jne 1's, middle and right, are 12'' tall. Larger doll has leather legs and feet. Smaller dolls have wood feet. (Dolls are shown dressed on Page 1.)

Some Bru on leather bodies had carved wood hands and wood lower legs and feet. These hands belong to a Nursing Bru.

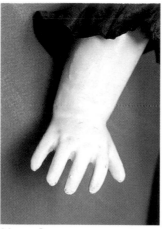

Many Steiners on composition bodies have short, stubby fingers all about the same length.

Some early Brus had wood bodies with wood hands. Fingers curled under.

Steiner Motschmann-type bodies had well-formed porcelain hands.

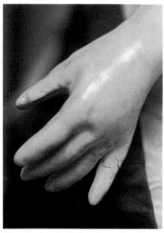

Papier-mâché hand from A9T is unusual.

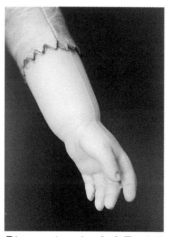

Bisque hand of A.T. doll. Hands were fitted into leather sleeve that completed lower arm.

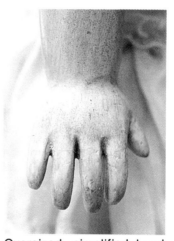

Oversized, simplified hand of Incised Jumeau was made of pressed wood.

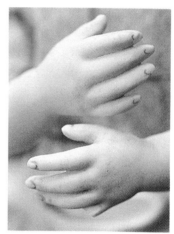

All bisque Bru hands, except those of Brevetés, seem to be from same mold. Nails are lightly outlined.

Bisque Marque hand is beautifully modeled. Hand and lower arm are one-piece, with ball-joint part of arm.

P.D. hands were painted metal. They seem small in proportion to P.D. dolls. Note wrist joint.

Wood hands on dolls marked *H* are well-shaped and graceful.

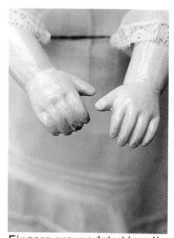

Fingers are modeled together on papier-mâché body. Head is unmarked.

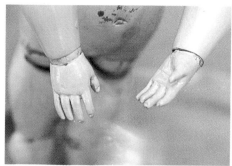

Huret doll has metal hands with joints at wrist.

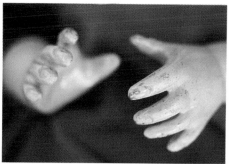

Schmitt composition hands have separate, short fingers. Nails are indented.

A.T. bisque hand on leather-body doll. Nails are outlined.

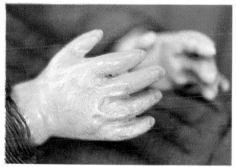

Wood hands on H-dolls are similar but vary in finger positions.

Early Long-Faced Jumeau has large, heavy hands that were well-designed and well-made.

Bru Brevetés had clawlike bisque hands. Nails were outlined.

Bisque hands on composition arms are found on this rare, wire-eyed, C-series Steiner. Jumeau was only other company that added bisque hands to composition arms.

Hands and Lower Arms—Doll hands and lower arms of large French dolls were made without a joint in the wrist. They were called *unjointed wrist, gauntlet-type arm* or *straight wrist.* Most French doll-making companies used the straight wrist before 1890. Then many French companies changed to the jointed wrist, which allowed the hand to be posed in a more natural position.

Some dolls' hands were distinguishable from hands of other doll makers. Hands of Steiner dolls had short, stubby fingers that were all the same length. Jumeau made hands extra large. Porcelain bisque hands were used, but not exclusively, by Bru, Jumeau and Steiner. Thuillier also used bisque hands.

The Jumeau and Steiner companies made bisque hands and lower arms that fitted into the elbow joints of a composition body. Dolls with these bisque arms are not common, but examples can be found in the Margaret Strong Museum in Rochester, New York.

Marque dolls have one-piece bisque hands and lower arms that fit into the joint of the composition upper arm. All Marque dolls are the same size and from the same mold, and all have the same beautifully modeled hands.

Bru Hands—Often, the first bisque hands we think of are the lovely, graceful, tinted hands of Bru dolls. Hands are in good proportion to the body, with separate fingers modeled in a relaxed pose. These hands were made in many sizes.

Bru arms came in two lengths. One arm was cut on a slant midway to the elbow. The other type of hand had a joint cast in the porcelain. This fitted into a pin-joint with a reinforced upper arm of leather over wood.

Bru made other bisque hands. The very early Bru Breveté has a claw-shaped hand with tinted cuticles. Fingers are thinner than those on Bru Jnes. All fingers are about the same length, and they are pointed. The forearms went midway to the elbow, where they were inserted into a leather sleeve to complete the arm.

A.T. Hands—Two different types of bisque hands were used on A.T. dolls made by Thuillier. On both types of hands, arms were cut off below the elbow and set into leather, which made the rest of the arm. Bisque hands on the Snow Angel (A7T) are the graceful, relaxed hands of a child. Another small A.T. has fingers bent up sharply, as if she were supposed to be carrying or holding something.

Steiner Hands—Early Steiners, with Motschmann-type bodies, had bisque arms that ended above the elbow. Arms had only a slight curve and hands pointed straight down. The arms were attached with strips of muslin or leather above the elbow.

Wood Hands—Wood hands and arms were sometimes used by Bru. The wood arms were pin-jointed into the upper arm, which was covered with leather. Wood hands and lower arms are sometimes found on the Nursing Bru. Differently shaped wood hands are found on some Bru composition bodies.

Occasionally we find a rare, all-wood body by Bru. One type of all-wood body has jointed wrists and ankles and wood hands. Another all-wood Bru body has wood hands with fingers curled under. We have this doll in our collection.

Jumeau made a hand from sawdust and glue. The H-doll has the most graceful wood arms and hands, with smooth-working joints in the arms.

Metal Hands—A few dolls were made with metal hands. In our collection, we have only three dolls with metal hands—two Petit and Dumontier (P.D.) dolls and a Huret doll. The two P.D. dolls have small metal hands, which are graceful but out of proportion with their bodies. The Huret doll has a flat metal hand, painted flesh color with no tinting.

DOLL FEET

We have found variation in the feet of French dolls. We feel certain that the person who originally bought a doll did not take off shoes and socks to see what feet looked like. Even a purchaser of an undressed doll probably didn't buy a doll because feet were well-modeled.

French dolls discussed in this book have feet made of wood, leather, papier-mâché, composition or bisque. Detail on feet had much to do with the material used to make them. Finer detail is possible in modeled bisque or carved wood than in other materials. Some materials, such as stuffed leather, didn't adapt themselves to fine detail shaping on toes and toenails.

We removed shoes and socks from many different dolls and compared the shape and detail of toes and feet. Feet of large, late Schmitt dolls were modeled differently than feet of early Schmitts. The big toe on late Schmitt dolls was separate, and there was some modeling on the bottom of the toes. There was a definite arch and a plump instep on late dolls.

Our oldest Schmitt has a flat foot with four toes. Nails are elongated, and the foot is ugly. The bottom of the foot was marked *1 ad R* in ink. Our early 12-inch Schmitt has a similar foot,

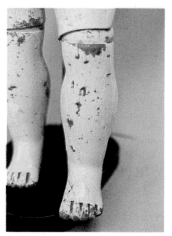

Solid wood legs on all-wood-body Bru are an unusual find.

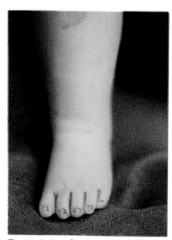

Porcelain foot on Motschmann-type Steiner dolls.

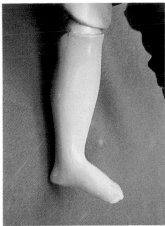

Marque foot is long, with little detail.

Unmarked papier-mâché foot is simple and well-shaped.

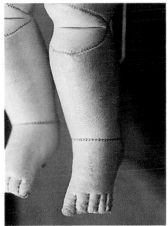

Leather feet with sewn toes on Bru Breveté are similar to those on Crescent Bru.

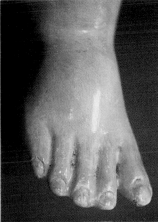

P.D. foot has nails outlined in red. Some P.D. dolls have only four toes.

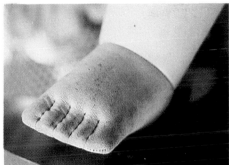

Fat leather foot from Crescent Bru. Toes are stitched in.

Steiner composition foot often has big toe modeled separately.

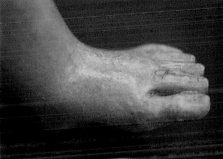

Interesting shape of foot from doll marked only *4H*. Foot is wood with carved arch and detailed toes.

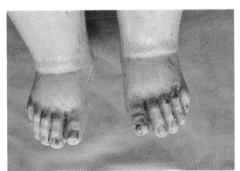

Wood F.G. feet from Gesland body.

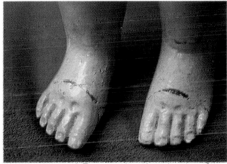

Wood feet of Bru on leather body often crack across toes because grain of wood is crosswise at that point.

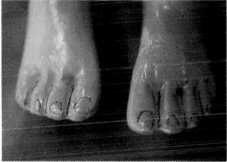

On Schmitt dolls, smaller toes extend beyond big toe. Feet usually have size number or ink markings on bottom.

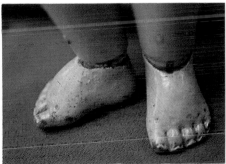

Wood feet of Huret doll have unusual ankle joints.

but on the side you can almost see another little toe. The bottom of this foot is marked *N o 12* in ink. A third early Schmitt has two words in script on the bottom of the foot, but we can't decipher them.

We have seen F.G. heads on many different bodies, but when we examined the feet of a marked Gesland composition body, we found a straight, flat foot with nails and toes modeled together. We believe we must consider the body markings to compare feet rather than the *F.G.* head marking.

One of our Long-Faced Jumeaus has a very old body with the ball of the knee joint fastened to the lower leg. On this Jumeau foot, the big toe is separate, and deep creases indicate other toes. There is some modeling of toenails, but the foot has no modeling on the bottom—it is flat.

The composition foot of one large SFBJ doll has toes modeled together and rounded, with little shaping. A large, incised *13* is found on the bottom of the right foot. Another SFBJ doll has a foot that is similar but without a number on the bottom.

We saw one large A-series Steiner with a separate big toe, but the toe was not bent up. There were no toenail indications, and the foot had no modeling on the bottom.

On our Bébé Steiner with straight legs, the big toe is the longest, and the other toes slant up to it. On a jointed Steiner, we found a foot shaped the same way.

A Circle and Dot Bru on a composition body has a foot with a flat bottom and no toenails, but toes are partially defined. This doll has an unusual roll of fat at the ankle.

When we checked our A.T. dolls, we found Nos. 8 and 11 have the same kind of feet but in different sizes. There is a suggestion of toes, and the foot is flat on the bottom.

The composition feet of the Marque doll are long and thin, with thin ankles. There is little modeling of the toes.

P.D. dolls have a simple, crudely modeled foot. The foot is longer and narrower than feet of most other dolls.

Many Bru dolls have wood feet, such as the Nursing Bru, the Bru Jne 5 and others. These wood feet were well-made with well-defined toes and an arch. We often find wood toes broken off Bru dolls because the crossgrain of the wood is weak.

A very rare Gourmand Bru, which advertisements of the time claimed could eat and digest food, has well-modeled, chubby, bisque baby legs and feet.

H-dolls have beautifully carved toes that are well-defined on the top and bottom of the foot. The foot also has a well-shaped arch.

Some of the most interesting wood feet we have found were on a fabric-covered Gesland body. We display this doll in our home without shoes or socks so everyone can see the wood feet. Toes are carefully carved, with joints indicated for each toe. There is an arch, and the foot has a narrow heel.

Another realistic wood foot is found on the all-wood-body Huret. Toes are defined on the top and bottom, and nails are well-shaped. The foot also has a joint at the ankle.

Leather feet, with sewn toes, are found on older Bru and Thuillier dolls. There is little detail in leather feet.

DOLL EARS

We have been making mold for over 40 years and are always conscious of the structure of ears on a doll. When deciding if we can make a mold of an antique head, the first thing we do is study mold lines and ears. If there is evidence the mold line runs up the head and under the ear, then the ear was applied *after* the head was cast.

When we look inside a head, we can also determine how ears were made. If there is no indentation in the casting where ears are, then we believe ears were applied or the head was pressed with paste (soft clay) to solidly fill the ear part of the mold.

We are concerned with ears because it can determine whether you get a good mold from a head or a broken head. If ears are applied, it is very difficult to make a mold over them because the original mold had no ears.

Ears that are big, solid lumps applied to the side of the head, like the Long-Faced Jumeau, are almost impossible to make a mold over. Dolls with less-obtrusive ears can have clay added at the ear so molds pull apart easily.

Right: Bru Breveté, 12 inches tall, is still in excellent condition. Body is unwarped and unsoiled, and label is still intact. Note clawlike bisque hands.

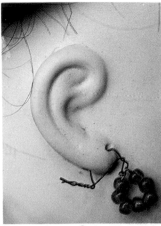

Ear on large Schmitt doll is well-shaped and was applied after head was cast.

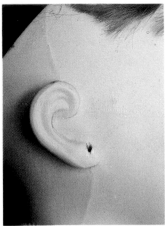

Applied A.T. ear. Only outer semicircle was applied to greenware head. Note mold line.

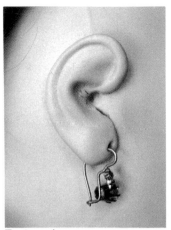

Early Jumeau ear was barely attached. An ear canal was made in porcelain greenware head.

Early Schmitt ear applied over mold marks on head.

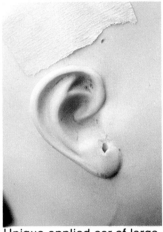

Unique applied ear of large, A-series Steiner. Center of ear was worked into head at greenware stage.

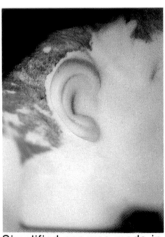

Simplified ear was made in mold of SFBJ.

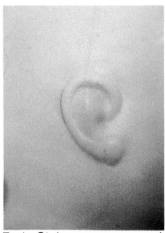

Early Steiner ears were set close to head, with little detail. Ears were made in the mold and not pierced.

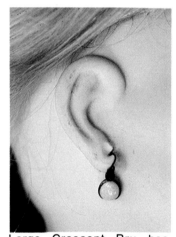

Large Crescent Bru has well-shaped, applied ears that are well-attached and modeled on head. Note original earring.

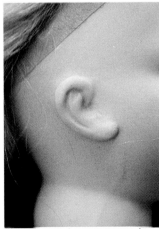

Huret ear is uneven along mold line. It was crudely modeled on head in greenware stage and is not pierced.

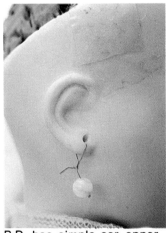

P.D. has simple ear, apparently made in mold. Fine brass-wire earrings will not damage bisque.

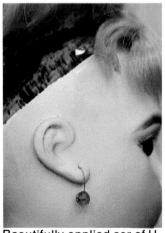

Beautifully applied ear of H-doll.

Older, unmarked French doll has lobe pulled away from head to make space for earring hole. Ears may have been modeled after application. Doll wears original earring.

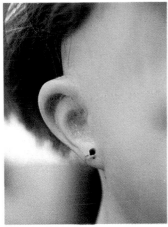

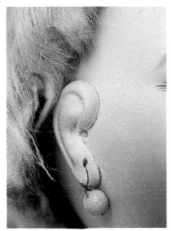

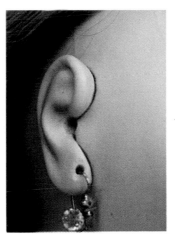

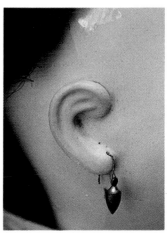

Pixielike ear of Marque doll was made in five-piece head mold.

Ear from Incised Jumeau is like flat patch. Tiny ear canal was added in front of ear.

Applied ear of Long-Faced Jumeau was probably one of earliest made, which accounts for its crudeness and poor application.

Phenix Bébé has neatly shaped, semicircular ear.

In this section, we are not concerned with making molds but with studying the structure of different ears. This knowledge may give you a clue to the age of a doll and its sculptor, or you may see a resemblance in ears of dolls made by the same company.

Ears often show the progress of a company. Sometimes they show how a company tried to economize by having one mold instead of a mold for the head and a mold for each ear. One complete mold allowed the company to eliminate the time spent applying ears. When companies changed from pressing molds to pouring molds with porcelain slip, it was easier to cast ears right on the head.

There are many more applied ears than generally believed. Applied ears were used on dolls of all sizes. The big, heavy applied ears of some early Jumeaus are easily recognized, even by novices, but the finely modeled C-shaped ears were also applied.

We do not make any generalizations about ear modeling, but we use the dolls in our collection to show examples. We can examine these doll heads inside and out.

A.T. Dolls—A.T. dolls, Nos. 9, 11 and 12, have neatly made, semicircular C-shaped ears, which were applied to the head and pierced through the lobe. All A.T. ears are similar in shape.

Jumeau Dolls—There is much variation in Jumeau ears. Our three Long-Faced Jumeaus have applied ears that are heavy, thick and barely attached. These are the most obvious of any applied ears.

The Incised Jumeau is another doll with thick ears. They were modeled in a heavy I-shape,

then applied to the doll's head.

The E.J. Jumeau has a thick, C-shaped, applied ear with a hole for a pierced earring. The ear of the Portrait Jumeau is very similar.

All ears of very early Jumeaus that we've examined have a round indentation for the ear canal. The similarity in modeling among Jumeau ears leads us to believe Carrier-Belleuse modeled all of them.

Bru Dolls—There is some variation in the ears of Brus. Our Bru Jne 8 has neatly applied, long, thin ears with a thick lobe. The Bru Jne 1 dolls have ears of the same shape. The top part of the ear of the Bru Jne 6 doll is tipped back. Ears are thick but delicate in appearance. The hole for a pierced earring is in the *top* of the lobe. Ears of all Circle and Dot Brus appear to have been made in the mold.

Other Dolls—We have only three H-dolls to examine, but their ears are similar. They have applied, half-heart-shaped ears with two softly modeled lines. The inner part of the ear has no modeling.

Ears of P.D. dolls lack detail and lie very close to the head. These ears were made in the head mold.

Ears of Marque dolls are unlike any other dolls'. They are like flaps—they stick out from the head in a pixielike way. These ears were made in the head mold.

We have only one Huret doll, and ears are applied over mold marks. We believe modeling on ears was done *after* ears were applied to the head. The ear shape has no deep indentations, and the outside is long instead of shaped like a half-circle.

Our Phenix Bébé has applied ears that stand away from her head. The ear has only an outer shell or outer shape, with no inner modeling on the head.

Ears on our large, A-series Steiner are carefully modeled and uniquely applied. The inner part of the ear is deeper than the surface of the head. Another A-series has a more simply shaped ear. A large, wire-eyed Steiner has applied ears that are well-worked into the head form and very delicately modeled. Steiners on Motschmann-type bodies have flat ears with no detail—these ears were made in the mold.

All F.G. heads we have examined had ears made in the mold. This is even true with our 32-inch doll.

Most later dolls, such as SFBJ dolls, had simplified ears, with very little detail. Ears were made in the mold as part of the head.

DOLL EYES, EYEBROWS AND EYELASHES

Eyes, eyebrows and eyelashes of French dolls are important because they help give each doll a personality. Photos will help you identify differences in eyes, eyebrows and eyelashes.

Some things are similar on all French dolls, such as the black edge around the inside of eye holes. This black line helps give depth to the eyes and enhances the face.

Eyelashes—Eyelashes were almost always painted black. The only exceptions are very early dolls, such as Schmitts and some Portrait Jumeaus, whose lashes were a lighter charcoal color. On all makes of dolls, lashes usually slant away from the nose. Later SFBJ dolls have real-hair lashes on the upper eyelid and bottom lashes that were painted straight down.

Eyebrows—Every doll-making company had a style of painting eyebrows. Some companies used two tones of the same color paint. Doll painters first painted the "shadow color" (underneath color) where the eyebrow should be. Then the painter stroked in the feathering over the top of the shadow to complete the brow. *Feathering* was made with single, fine strokes of a brush or quill. These fine lines were painted in a particular pattern or style.

We can often tell which company made a doll by looking at the feathering on eyebrows. As you study the photographs in this book, you will see what we mean. You must be aware that as time passed and new directors became part of a company, artwork changed. The Bru Co. is one example of this. Early Brus had soft, natural-

Bru has soft brows and many fine, even lashes.

SFBJ No. 247 has sleep eyes, real lashes on upper lid and painted lashes on lower lid.

Later Schmitt dolls have wider, softer brows and numerous, evenly spaced lashes.

A7T has soft, feathered brows and light eyelashes.

E.D. dolls often have brows that almost touch. There is no lid indentation, so lashes are soft and light.

Bru Jne 7 has heavy black line around eye to help cover bad fit. Brows are soft and dull.

Bru Jne R9 has black shiny eyebrows painted with harsh lines.

Nursing Bru has misplaced, mismatched eyebrows.

Unmarked Belton-type doll with unevenly cut eyes. Brows are dark and strongly feathered.

Narrow brow and almond-shaped cobalt eyes of very early Steiner

Incised Jumeau has unevenly cut eye holes. Note heavy eye shadow.

Long-Faced Jumeaus may have mismatched eyebrows, as this one. Early Jumeaus had mauve eye shadow.

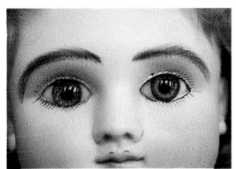

Wire-eyed, A-series Steiner has square cut out of rim of head for eye mechanism.

Doll marked F.C.G. has brows that are different than dolls marked F.G. in scroll. We assume, from recent research, both dolls were made by Francois Gaultier.

Dolls marked F.G. in scroll have brows painted line-on-line. When lashes were painted, brush skipped over lid indentation.

Early Schmitt head has thin brows and mauve eye shadow on pale bisque.

Early Steiner, made before 1885, has almond-shaped eyes, narrow brows and eye shadow.

1-H doll has soft, lightly feathered brows. Lashes are short and pale. A little eye shadow was used, and eyes have radiating lines.

looking eyebrows. Later Brus, made after 1892, had dark eyebrows, with gloss added to the paint.

Eyes—French Bébés usually had paperweight eyes in blue or brown. Occasionally, some dolls were made with gray eyes. We even have a 32-inch Jumeau with green eyes.

The crystal on the front of the eyes of Bébés varies in thickness, which gives them different depths. Later, when French doll-making companies began experimenting with sleep eyes, the companies could not use eyes with a bulge of crystal because they would not close.

DOLL TEETH

For many years, we have searched for definitive information to establish a manufacturing date for French dolls with two rows of teeth. Teeth are little and appear almost pointed, and many doll collectors refer to them as *fish teeth*.

We have owned three A.T. dolls that had two rows of little teeth. The first doll was 28 inches tall and had inferior painting, which was an indication of when the doll was made. We believed this doll was older than closed-mouth A.T. dolls. We also had a large, lady A.T. doll of fine bisque, with delicate painting, that had the same tiny teeth in two rows.

We have a small A4T with unusual teeth. She has three teeth on top and three on the bottom, with one tooth centered on the top and one on the bottom. The other two A.T. dolls with teeth had more teeth than could naturally be in the mouth of a doll. These teeth are similar to the old bamboo ones of Oriental dolls, copied by Motschmann.

At a Theriault auction in May, 1983, an R.D.3 (Rabery and Delphieu) doll was sold. It was dated by the Theriaults at around 1885, and it had two rows of tiny teeth.

Jumeau made a mechanical doll that had a movable head and arms. The head was marked *Déposé Tete Jumeau Bte S.G.D.G.*, and had two rows of tiny teeth.

There seem to be many Steiners with unusual sets of teeth. The crying-and-kicking Steiner is well-known, and her open mouth with two rows of teeth is familiar to many doll collectors. We also have a swivel-head Steiner with pointed teeth.

Fish teeth on old, kicking Steiner.

We have read in many books that Motschmann copied the body and teeth of an Oriental doll from an exhibit held in 1857. Today we wonder if Steiner copied the same body and teeth, or did he copy Motschmann? We believe part of the fun of learning about dolls is not being able to figure out everything.

We thought dolls with many tiny upper and lower teeth were a very early version of Bébés with teeth. The only date we have located was the mention of Jumeau experiments with open mouth and teeth in 1888 in the magazine *LaNature*.

Research has shown us if Jumeau was doing something, other companies were probably doing the same thing. The teeth of later Jumeaus, and most other French dolls, changed around the end of the 19th century. Doll makers used only upper teeth that were more natural looking.

Putting Teeth in Doll's Head—Teeth were put in a doll head in one of three ways. They were made separately and added in the greenware stage, they were modeled in the doll's mouth or they were made separately and glued in a finished head.

Right: Doll is incised E12J Déposé. Most E.J. dolls are good additions to collections. Arm sockets are worn, but otherwise doll is in original condition.

Many SFBJ dolls had teeth modeled in an open-closed mouth. These included the Laughing Jumeau and the Twirp. We saw a set of Jumeau character dolls in Ralph's Doll Museum in Parksville, Missouri, with wide-open mouths and well-formed teeth. Another Jumeau doll, with an open mouth and two rows of teeth, was sold at a Theriault auction in 1982. Jumeau character dolls with teeth are scarce but do occasionally appear.

In 1983, a character Jumeau with teeth sold at Sotheby Auctions in London. The doll looked Oriental and had six upper teeth and four lower ones. She had a wide-open, laughing mouth.

A few unmarked dolls have two rows of teeth in an open-closed mouth, with no actual opening into the head. One is the Lanternier doll.

After 1900, many French dolls were made with open mouths and teeth. These dolls were harder to produce, but they were made to compete with German dolls. German dolls had been made with open mouths and teeth since around 1890.

As we studied the insertion of teeth in many French dolls, we have changed our conclusion on the approximate time they were made, especially A.T.s. We conclude that tiny teeth set into the mouths of A.Ts was the result of the company's changing from closed to open mouths, probably in the mid-1890s. This would be *after* the time Thuillier made dolls. Another company was probably using his molds. Most dolls with teeth were made after 1900.

We have proof Steiner was the first to produce dolls with open mouths with two rows of teeth. His Motschmann-type dolls have this type of mouth and teeth, and they were made as early as 1860.

In January 1984, a Steiner doll with an open, laughing mouth and two rows of teeth was sold at a Theriault auction. She was dated by the Theriaults at around 1885.

A 21-inch Tête Jumeau, incised *10* and stamped with a blue *Bébé Jumeau* body stamp, was sold at a Sotheby Auction in the summer of 1983. The doll had six tiny upper teeth and real eyelashes. Because she had real eyelashes, it would establish her date at 1895 or after.

There are other dolls with modeled teeth, and some are very early dolls. Crescent or Circle and

We finally found a F1 (Figure) B11 Steiner, with 2 rows of teeth and wire eyes. 18".

Dot Brus had teeth modeled in the open-closed mouth, but usually these teeth are painted with lip color. When painted black, the Crescent Bru has painted white teeth. A Crescent Bru doll exhibiting this type of painting is on display at the Margaret Strong Museum in Rochester, New York.

If you look closely at the modeling on many French Bébés with closed mouths, you will see a tiny rim of upper teeth modeled in. This is commonly referred to by dealers as "the best models with a tongue between their lips." Look more closely—is it a tongue or the place where teeth would naturally be? Look at Brus, A.T.s, H-dolls and other closed-mouth French dolls, then you decide.

Collectors should realize the closed-mouth Bébé is the best buy for investment purposes. Many collectors add open-mouthed Bébés to their collection because they are less expensive. Others collect dolls with open mouths and teeth because they find the dolls amusing. Some people collect Bébés with teeth for historical reasons.

In this section, we have attempted to call your attention to the details of doll faces and doll bodies. We have done this so you will be aware

Left: Incised *Dru Jne 5*, this rare 18-inch doll has an all-wood body.

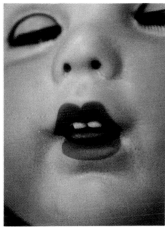

Open mouth with wobbly tongue of SFBJ No. 241.

Open-closed mouth of SFBJ No. 235.

Open mouth of SFBJ No. 238.

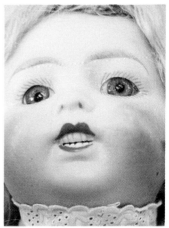

Open mouth with two rows of teeth. Doll is unmarked but Limoges is usually given credit for it.

Bru, marked with crescent, two concentric circles and dot. She is also marked *Bru Jne 11* and has molded teeth that were painted.

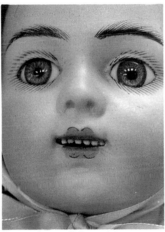

Bru Jne R9 with open mouth has six tiny teeth on top.

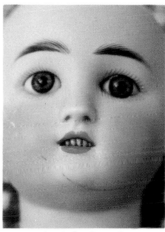

Unmarked Steiner has two rows of pointed teeth, sometimes called *fish teeth.*

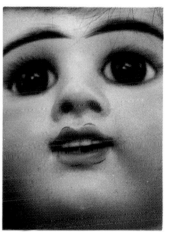

E.D. with smiling mouth and natural-looking teeth.

A.T. with open mouth and two rows of separate, tiny teeth.

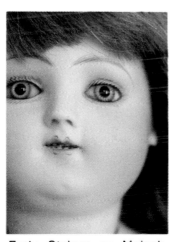

Early Steiner on Motschmann-type body has open mouth, four teeth on top and four teeth on bottom.

Black Crescent Bru with painted teeth.

Jumeau with mouthful of teeth photographed at Strong Museum in New York.

Left: Laughing Character Jumeaus. No. 208.

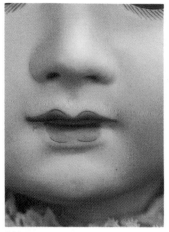

3H-doll has light line between slightly parted lips to indicate teeth.

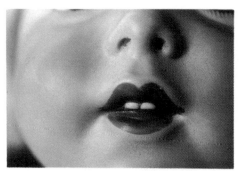

Open-closed mouth of SFBJ No. 247.

Open-closed mouth of SFBJ No. 236.

A4T with three teeth on top and three teeth on bottom.

Large doll, marked *F.G.* in scroll, has row of teeth modeled in mouth under upper lip. Teeth are painted with lip color.

Long-Faced Jumeau has white lines between parted lips to indicate teeth.

of small differences. Your knowledge and understanding will give you a greater appreciation for your own collection and the collection of others. It will also allow you to be more aware of details when you are studying a doll or when you are considering purchasing a Bébé.

DOLL MARKINGS

The majority of French Bébés are marked with initials or name of the doll maker stamped or incised on the back of necks or heads. These marks are as important as an artist's signature on a painting. Dolls made 100 years ago are hard to identify without them, and marked dolls are better investments than unmarked ones.

Some doll-making companies, such as the Jumeau Co., made two grades of dolls and sold them at different prices. The less-expensive Jumeau doll was unmarked.

Some very old dolls were unmarked for two reasons. First, doll makers made heads for other porcelain companies, so they left the doll head unmarked. Second, some doll makers did not consider it important to mark their dolls.

We are always learning about markings on dolls. Recent information leads us to believe dolls marked *PG* or *PBG*, which often are sold as Bru dolls, are probably not Brus. We now believe these dolls were made by Pintel and Godchaux.

Body Markings—Markings on bodies are also important. They often provide a date when the doll was made, as well as the name of the company that made the body. When body markings match head markings, it indicates the head is on the correct body.

Studying Markings—The following six pages show and explain the different markings you may find on French Bébé heads and bodies. Study them so you will be familiar with marks. One of your goals as an informed collector is to be able to recognize different marks of the various doll-making companies.

Right: Close-up of doll shows her sleep eyes, real lashes and open-closed mouth.

Head Markings and Body Labels

1

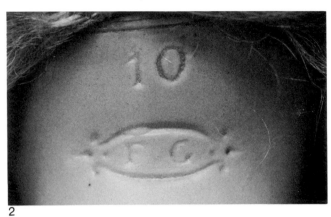

2

3

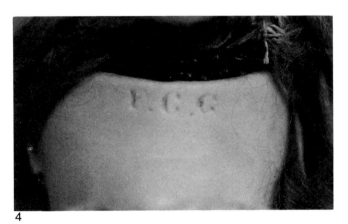

4

5

1. Gesland red-and-black label found on composition body with F.G. head. Proves he made composition bodies.
2. Incised *F.G.* for François Gaultier.
3. Incised *F.3.G* for François Gaultier.
4. Incised *F.C.G*, probably for François Gaultier.
5. Label found on stockinette body by Gesland with *F.G.* on head.
6. Body label, probably doll shop's, found on small Schmitt.

6

1

2

3

4

5

6

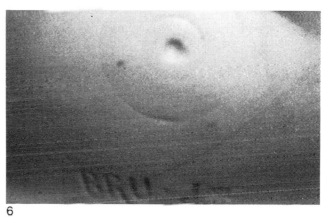

7

1. Incised mark from back of porcelain eye used to encase glass pupil for wire-eyed Steiners.

2. Incised *SIE C 5* for Steiner, C-series, size 5.

3. *SIE C 2/0.* Lever on left moves wire eyes. Steiner and Bourgoin names often found on wire-eyed Steiners.

4. Steiner Paris incised with F A Figure, size 11. This is one of many head marks used by J. Steiner.

5. Steiner label used before 1889, usually found on wire-eyed dolls.

6. Indented crescent with two concentric circles and dot was used by Bru. *Bru Jne 11* is incised beneath circles.

7. Paper body label for Bébé Bru Breveté.

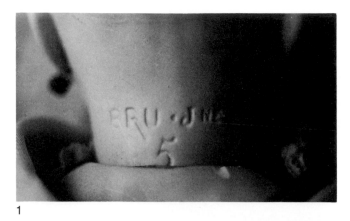

1

2

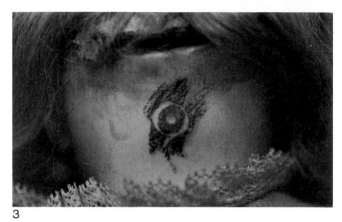

3

4

5

6

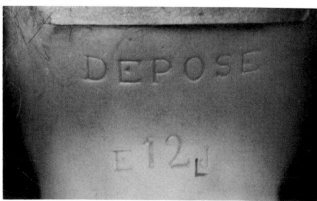

7

1. Incised marks on back of Bru Jne 5 head.
2. Paper body label from chest of Bru doll with wood legs.
3. Only mark on Circle and Dot Bru.
4. Kiss-throwing Bru Jne R was made after 1890.
5. *France SFBJ 247 Paris* was used by SFBJ company. Note holes for tying sleep eyes for shipping.
6. Jumeau stamped in red with *Déposé Tête Jumeau. Bte S.D.G.G* means registered. *4* is size. *L M 17* are tick marks or check marks. Hole originally had key that opened and closed eyes.
7. *E 12 J,* mark of Emile Jumeau. Red *L* is tick mark; 12 the size number.

1

2

3

4

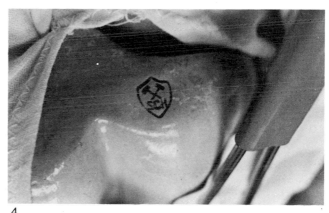

5

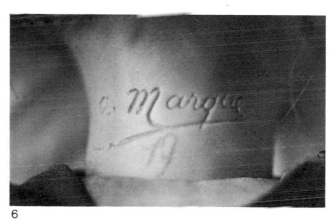

6

7

1. Body sticker found on composition Jumeau bodies.
2. Incised Déposé Jumeau used early by Jumeau. Dolls are referred to as *Incised Jumeaus*.
3. Red stamp of Tête Jumeau. Dolls with this stamp are most collected of all Jumeau dolls.
4. Black crossed hammers in shield body stamp of Schmitt.
5. Incised crossed hammers in shield used on back of head of Schmitt dolls.
6. Incised signature on Albert Marque doll heads.
7. Two Cs, back to back, is mark of unknown doll maker.

1

2

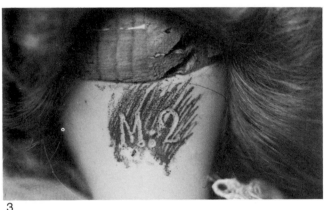

3

4

5

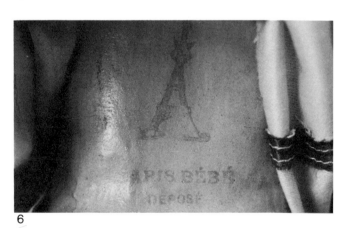

6

1. *E* and *9 D* in relief and incised *Déposé*. There is still a question about who produced E.D. dolls.
2. Crude, hand-incised mark, *A 11 T,* for A. Thuillier.
3. Tiny Mascotte doll with only *M.* and *2* incised. Made by May Brothers.
4. Letters for *A8T* have been pressed with stamp. This could be later A.T. doll.
5. Incised *P.2.D* for Petit and Dumontier.
6. Eiffel Tower body stamp of Paris Bébé made by Danel and Co.
7. Red head stamp used on Paris Bébé.

7

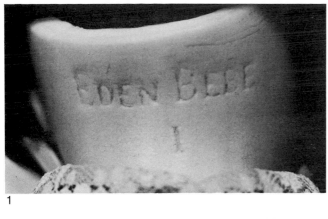

1

2

3

4

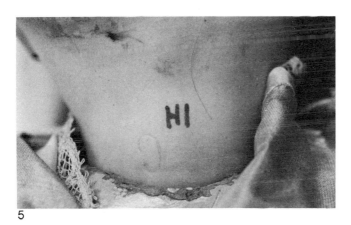

5

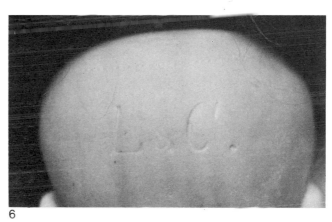

6

7

1. Eden Bebé incised by Fleischmann & Blödel.
2. Incised *Jullien* by Jullien.
3. *4 H* incised near rim of head by H. Halopeau.
4. Incised star and *94* of Phenix Bébé.
5. *H 1* in black china paint, incised *9* by unknown maker. This is *not* mark of H-dolls collectors search for. This might be a Portrait Jumeau, and *H 1* are tick marks.
6. Mark of *L&C.* Belton-type head has three holes. Doll could possibly be LeComte, Leconte, or H. Leconte & Co. of Paris.
7. Incised *R.3.D* for Rabery and Delphieu.

Putting It
All Together

BE YOUR OWN APPRAISER

It is a must for you to know the monetary value of dolls in your collection. If you're going to give them to a grandchild or donate them to a museum, you need to know how much they're worth. If dolls are to be sold at auction or if you want to sell them privately, you need to know values. You also need to know values for insurance purposes. And it's always fun to watch the prices of your dolls change.

Prices of dolls constantly change. Sometimes a doll is priced high, then the price stabilizes as more dolls of that kind are put into circulation. For instance, in 1984, P.D. dolls, made by Petit and Dumontier, were priced very high because they were rare and few collectors had them. Prices for P.D. dolls may stabilize, but there is no way to predict it. Other dolls, such as Schmitt dolls, have been priced high because they are hard to find.

Collectors of French dolls often want to enhance their collections by adding more dolls, selling some or trading dolls with other collectors. Every two or three years, or at least every five years for large collections, you must update the value of your dolls.

You can be your own appraiser by using price guides and other publications. Guides are printed about every two years. Be sure the one you use is not more than a year old. It takes at least a year to accumulate prices and get a book in print. So realize the prices you find in price guides may not be the most-current prices.

Some authors of price guides allow for this and estimate prices will increase by a certain percentage, such as 10%, by the time the book is in print. But the estimation of increase by an author of a price guide can be wrong. Prices might go down, or they might remain the same. Use price guides to give you a *general idea*, and use several guides to compare prices.

You can purchase auction catalogs with prices actually paid for dolls. Actual prices from these catalogs are the best gauge we have of the value of a doll at a given time.

Left: 18" wood bodied Bru Jne 5. She wears old wool challis dress trimmed with lace.

Prices of dolls advertised in magazines are "asking prices." You don't know if the seller received his asking price or if the doll was ever sold.

HOW TO APPRAISE YOUR OWN DOLL

To appraise your own doll, place the doll on a bed or other padded surface. Use the sample appraisal sheet below to help you appraise your doll. You may use this form or modify it to suit your needs.

Many people keep a record like this on their dolls, and it is easily updated. A loose-leaf notebook with separate sheets is good for keeping records on many different dolls.

If you wish to sell the doll yourself, make

DOLL APPRAISAL

For this example, we use a Jumeau doll.

Doll _FRENCH JUMEAU_   Doll's name _BROWN BETTY_

Maker _E. JUMEAU_   Marks on head _E 6 J_

Body marks _STAMP MEDAL D'OR_

Approximate date doll was made _1895_

Materials _HEAD-BISQUE/BODY-COMPOSITION_   Size _HEIGHT-22 INCHES_

Type _CHILD DOLL_   Mouth _CLOSED_

Eyes _BROWN PAPERWEIGHT_   Wig _ORIGINAL, BLACK MOHAIR_

Clothes _REDRESSED IN SILK, 1983_   Shoes _ORIGINAL, MARKED E.J._

General condition of doll _VERY GOOD_

List cracks, repairs, replacement body parts, repainting. (This is very important in adjusting value up or down)

DOLL HAS BOTH EAR LOBES CHIPPED, SHOWING WHITE BISQUE. ONE KNEE JOINT BROKEN AND REPAIRED. REPAIRED SECTION WAS REPAINTED.

Purchase price of doll, year _DOLL WAS GIFT — NO PURCHASE PRICE_

List anything special about the doll that could make her special or more valuable _JUMEAU BROWN BISQUE HEAD AND BROWN COMPOSITION BODY ARE RARE._

Dates that pertain to doll _PURCHASED BY GRANDMOTHER IN 1896 OR 1897._

List price from at least two price guides. Give date and name of book. Check size and special features in prices guides. _$6,000 TO $6,500, 4TH BLUE BOOK, DOLLS & VALUES BY JAN FOULKE. NO BLACK FRENCH LISTED._

Find doll, or similar doll, in current auction prices. _THERIAULT AUCTION CATALOG $8,500._

Current value _$8,500._

copies of your appraisals. Send copies to doll dealers and doll clubs, or give one to people who might wish to purchase the doll. This makes it easy to provide accurate information, and you won't forget important facts. If you give copies to people, you may not want to include how much you paid for the doll. Just put a piece of paper over this item when making copies.

If you want to sell the doll by a written advertisement or if you wish to add a description to your insurance papers, summarize information as shown below. It's also good to have a photo of the doll to go with each description or appraisal. Below is a summarization of information found on the doll appraisal sheet on the previous page.

French, bisque, brown child doll, 22 inches.
Socket head.
Brown, paperweight eyes.
Long, painted lashes and feathered brows.
Closed mouth.
Chipped, pierced ears.
Black-mohair wig.
Jointed, brown composition body with knee repair and straight wrists.
Marked *E6J* and body stamp.
Recently costumed in striped silk.
Shoes original and marked.
Made by E. Jumeau around 1895.

BOOKS AND MAGAZINES
FOR DOLL COLLECTORS

Boehm, Max. *Dolls*. New York: Dover, 1972.
Coleman, Dorothy, Elizabeth and Evelyn. *The Collector's Encyclopedia of Dolls*. New York: Crown Publishers, 1968.
Davies, Nina S. *The Jumeau Doll Story*. Washington, D.C.: Hobby House, 1957.
Foulk, Jan. *Dolls and Values, 4th Blue Book*, Cumberland, MD.: Holly House Press, 1980. (This is one of a series.)
King, Constance Eileen. *Jumeau*. Cumberland, MD: Hobby House Press, 1983.
King, Constance Eileen. *The Collector's History of Dolls*. New York: St. Martins, 1977.
Noble, Jon. *Beautiful Dolls*. New York: Hawthorne Books, 1971.
Seeley, Mildred and Colleen. *Doll Collecting for Fun and Profit*. Livonia, MI: Scott Publications.
Seeley, Mildred and Colleen. *Doll Costuming*. Livonia, MI: Scott Publications
St. George, Eleanor. *The Dolls of Yesterday*. New York: Scribner's, 1948.
White, Gwen. *European and American Dolls*. New York: Crescent Books, 1966.
Whitton, Margaret. *The Jumeau Story*. New York: Dover, 1980.

Right: 23-inch A11T has a character face. She is a good investment doll and a joy to own.

Glossary

Angora—Soft hair from goat used for early doll wigs.

Antique Doll—Doll over 75 years old.

Applied Ears—Ears of doll not included in head mold but made in separate mold and added to head in greenware stage.

Articulate—Manner in which bodies and limbs were joined to provide movement.

Ball-Joints—Round wood bead used in joint to facilitate movement.

Bébé—Doll made to represent French child.

Belton—Early partner of Jumeau, but no connection to bald-headed dolls has been found.

Belton-Type—Doll with closed head that is flattened or rounded. Head may have one or three holes.

Bisque—Porcelain clay fired to vitrification.

Black Light—Type of bulb used with dolls to see repairs through bisque. Other uses include to show minerals or to attract insects.

Blown Eyes—Round glass eyes with stem where blow pipe was broken off. Eye looks like tiny Christmas ball. Used mainly in German dolls and dolls with sleep eyes.

Blush—Rosy color applied as cheek color or over eyes as shadow.

Breveté—Patented. *Bte* is abbreviated form used on some dolls.

Carton-Pate—Pasteboard.

Cat's Tongue—Type of brush used for painting mouths on dolls.

Ceramic—Any fired clay product.

Character Dolls—Lifelike representation of real children.

Chemise—Plain dress doll wore when it was sold; undergarment covering top part of body.

China Clay—Fine white clay.

China Mop—Large round brush with soft bristles used to apply face blush on dolls.

Closed Mouth—Doll with lips modeled together.

Collectable Doll—Doll between 35 and 75 years old.

Composition—Material (paper pulp, glue, wood chips, sawdust or grain) used to make doll bodies. Harder than papier-mâché.

Cone—Commercially made pyramid of clay that melts at exact temperature. Used for testing kiln temperatures.

Contemporary Clothing—Clothing made within 10 years of time doll was made, but *not* doll's original clothes.

Cork—Substance used for pates of many French dolls.

Croquill Pen—Art pen used today to paint lashes on reproduction dolls.

Cuvets—Cuplike wood pieces inserted in legs and arms to make joints work better. Also used as reinforcement.

D.E.P.—Means déposé in French; deponier in German.

Déposé—Mark on doll's head, which means *registered*.

Doll's Markings—Doll's birthmark or company identification letters, size and mold numbers.

Double-Jointed—Another term for ball-jointed.

Fabricant—Manufacturer of dolls.

Feathering—Fine lines of eyebrow.

Fire—Heat clay to vitrification.

Flux—Glasslike substance that makes colors flow when melted with heat. Also makes colors glossy.

Gazette—Porcelain screen or rack. Wafer of unfired porcelain is placed on screen or rack, along with greenware heads, for firing.

Gesland—Company that made knit-covered, stuffed doll bodies, with metal armature, and composition doll bodies.

Greenware—Unfired porcelain shape made by pouring slip into mold.

Gussets—Joint in leather or cloth body made by adding separate oval piece of material.

Hairline Crack—Tiny crack in bisque.

Hundles—Flat, woven baskets that doll heads were dried in.

Hydrocal—Very hard plaster used to make master molds.

Incassable—Unbreakable.

Incised—Indented into, as numbers pressed into unfired bisque.

Left: Our 23-inch Bru Jne 10 has composition body. Her brown eyes are blushed above lids. She wears antique white-cotton dress.

Iris—Colored part of eye.

Jne—Jeune, Junior.

Kaolin Vats—Large wood tubs in which clay was left to soak in preparation for making doll heads.

Kaolin—Pure-white clay used for making dolls.

Kiln—Furnace designed to heat clay objects to vitrification. Wood was used to heat most old doll kilns, but modern kilns are electric.

Kissing Doll—Right arm and hand raise to touch lips and throw a kiss. Put into action by pulling string.

Lignite—Decayed vegetation, often found in prepared porcelain slips.

Master Mold—Mold used to produce other molds. Originally made of hydrocal but now made of rubber.

Mildew—Dark spots that appear on finished ware, usually caused when porcelain is underfired.

Milettes—Small French dolls under 14 inches tall.

Milvex—Type of colored composition developed by us for making reproduction doll bodies.

Mint—When applied to dolls, it means "unplayed-with" condition.

Mohair — Soft luxurious hair from the Angora goat. Used for doll wigs.

Motschmann—Doll bodies with porcelain sections joined together by leather or muslin. Steiner's Motschmann-type bodies are most well-known. He designed body after seeing Oriental dolls made that way.

Open-Closed Mouth—Lips parted as if open, but no opening in bisque.

Original—Artist's modeled doll or doll head used to make mold.

Oval Eyes—Similar to paperweight eyes, but no crystal added over pupil. Used mainly in antique lady dolls and some very early Steiner dolls.

Palette Knife—Small, flat knife, similar to spreader, used by painters.

Paperweight Eyes—Almond-shaped eye with bulge over eyeball of crystal.

Papier-Mâché—Combination of paper pulp and glue. Used to make doll bodies, doll heads and other toys.

Paste—Old term used for soft clay pressed in molds.

Left: Side view of doll's face shows the crystal bulge over paperweight eyes. Crystal bulge gives paperweight eyes depth and beauty.

Pate—Cork or other substance used to round top of head where bisque was cut off.

Plaster Mold—Reverse form of doll made of plaster of Paris used to duplicate shape. Doll heads were produced by pouring molds with liquid clay.

Pompadore—Red paint used to give rosiness to cheeks and lips. Used on antique and reproduction dolls.

Porcelain Slip—Form of liquid clay made by adding water to porcelain. Slip is poured into molds. This replaced method of pressing paste clay in molds.

Potassium Silicate—Chemical added to wood chips to make doll's hands hard and less breakable. Used by Jumeau.

Pounce—Wad of wool inside china-silk covering used to apply cheek color to porcelain dolls with a light, gentle up-and-down dabbing motion.

Pupil—Black center of doll eye.

Relief—Built up, as numbers on head raised above surface.

Reproduction—*Exact* copy. Doll made in mold made from old doll, with identical painting.

Scrubbie—Product with sponge on one side and rough sandpaperlike substance on other side. Used to clean and polish bisque.

Shadow Color—Color applied first to eyebrow section of doll. Feathering is added on top of color.

Straight Wrists—Also called *gauntlet-type wrists* or *unjointed wrists*. Hand and forearm without joint.

Swivel Neck—Head that turns in socket.

Synite—One ingredient of porcelain.

Terra Cotta—Fired red clay.

Undercuts—Indentations that keep mold from pulling off clay model.

Vitrification—Bringing clay to point of chemical change from where it can never be returned to clay.

Voice Box—Any mechanism installed in doll for making sounds.

Warp—To become misshapened in firing process.

Whiteware—Old term for fired porcelain or bisque.

Wig—Hair arrangement on doll.

Wire-Eyed—Eyes that open and close by use of lever behind ear or with controls in back of head. Steiner dolls with wire-eyed mechanism are most well-known.

About the Authors

Mildred and Vernon Seeley have been involved in doll making and doll collecting for nearly 40 years. They were the former owners of Seeley's Ceramics. Both are noted authorities on doll making, antique doll appraising and doll photography. Together, they also work as consultants to doll businesses, give lectures and hold seminars on antique dolls.

Mildred has studied art, sculpture and painting. She holds a master's degree in art education. She has written numerous books on dolls and doll making and was the founder of the Doll Artisan Guild. Vernon is a master mold maker and has made hundreds of molds from antique dolls. He holds degrees in science and industrial arts. He has written a textbook on ceramics and co-authored several doll books with Mildred.